D0283795

IN JAPAN
THE
CRICKETS
CRY

RONALD CLEMENTS
& STEVE METCALF

MONARCH
B O O K S
Oxford, UK & Grand Rapids, Michigan, USA

First published in the UK in 2010 by Monarch Books
(a publishing imprint of Lion Hudson plc)
Wilkinson House, Jordan Hill Road, Oxford OX2 8DR, England
Tel: +44 (0)1865 302750 Fax: +44 (0)1865 302757
Email: monarch@lionhudson.com
www.lionhudson.com

ISBN 978 1 85424 970 8

Distributed by:
UK: Marston Book Services, PO Box 269, Abingdon, Oxon, OX14 4YN
USA: Kregel Publications, PO Box 2607, Grand Rapids, Michigan 49501

British Library Cataloguing Data
A catalogue record for this book is available from the British Library.

Printed and bound in the UK by JF Print Ltd.

Blessed are the peacemakers,
for they will be called sons of God.

Matthew 5:9, NIV

For the people who,
through the last fifty-seven years,
have supported Evelyn and me
with their prayers and their gifts.

Steve

Contents

Acknowledgments

I am grateful to a number of people who have made this a better book. High on the list are my wife, Anne, and our daughters, Bethan, Emma and Shona, for patiently reading the manuscripts and encouraging me with variations on "Get it done!" and "Yes, you can!". Bethan also expertly wielded her editor's pen, challenging her father to justify everything from content to composition, and adding numerous commas.

Estelle Horne and Neil Yorkston kindly provided both material for and comments on my portrayal of life at Chefoo School and in Japanese internment. Keiko Holmes gave me valuable insights into her personal story and the reconciliation work of her organization, *Agape*. Andrew Alford and Miho Walker acted as reviewers of the book, making many useful suggestions which have enhanced the telling of Steve's story. Nathaniel Sonoda helped me with the Japanese characters. I am grateful to OMF UK for their initial approach, asking me to write this book; to Rebecca Brooker, OMF Books Publishing Manager, for her assistance; and to Monarch for putting it onto bookshelves. OMF UK also allowed me access to their archives and those held at the School of Oriental and African Studies.

Finally, my sincere thanks to Steve and Evelyn for allowing me to write this book. Steve has been incredibly patient and generous as I have negotiated my way around the many events of his life, asked more questions than I had a right to and probed for detail after detail after detail.

I do not know what impressions you will be left with as you read Steve's story, but for me, this book is a baton which we are passing on to you, and we pray that you will, in turn, pass its messages of forgiveness and reconciliation on to others.

Ronald Clements
August 2010

Biographee's Note

In 2003 I was speaking at a reconciliation meeting in Japan, and after I sat down two different Christian publishers came up to me asking for my story. Just over a year later my story was published in Japanese. The encouragement and blessing that resulted from that little book has added a whole new dimension to my missionary life.

I want to thank Dr Ronald Clements; he has gone out of his way and worked long hours in writing this book. We have become good friends as we have discussed my life and work and I trust you are blessed by his labour of love.

My hope and prayer is that this English biography may give its readers an insight into Japan – a prosperous and talented nation, but one that is still a great spiritual vacuum. Many nations in the East are seeing a spiritual awakening, but not Japan.

Much has changed since I first stepped from the Taiping onto Japanese soil. The population of 86 million has now increased to 127 million. Japanese communities live in almost every corner of the world. Japanese churches have grown in number and Japanese Christians are moving into leadership. But congregations remain small and Christians too few and far between. Japan remains a nation that needs you to become involved, sharing with the people the life-changing experience of God's constraining love. This is what I did sixty years ago. I never have had any regrets.

Stephen A. Metcalf
August 2010

ALMOST ALL MEN ARE MARKED IN SOME WAY BY THE
EXPERIENCE OF TAKING PART IN ANY WAR.

MAX HASTINGS[1]

There is an unconquered griminess to war. Marks not easily removed. Stains that linger through a lifetime. In conflict, graceful lines and form are deliberately destroyed. Images of twisted metal, of shattered concrete, become similes of damage done to men and to women – to aggressors and victims alike. We see it all the time. True reconciliation seems, at best, hard to achieve, frequently impossible.

Conflict and war darkened my childhood. The son of missionary parents, I was raised within reach of Chinese bandits who were the scourge of the local peasants. My boyhood was spent beneath the shadow of Japan's belligerent occupation of China. Aged fourteen, I became a civilian prisoner of war under the scrutiny of Japanese guards. Four years later I escaped this orbit of aggression and went to Australia. And there I understood that my life would complete a different circle. I must go to Japan and proclaim reconciliation for the Japanese and eternal peace with God.

巣立ち
Sudachi
(Leave Home)

Life, for me, had a precarious start.

I was born on 23 October 1927. Just a few weeks later, a disgruntled mob of army deserters ransacked the tribal village of Taku[2] in south-west China. This was the remote mountain home of my parents, Eddie and Bessie Metcalf, and the Eastern Lisu people,[3] among whom they worked. The men came down the hillside after dusk. Home after home was set on fire. A terrified Lisu young man scooped up Ruth, my four-year-old sister, and fled for the deep wooded gullies below the village. My father grabbed me, and he and my mother raced after the young man into the thicket. My mother shrieked as a bullet brushed the brim of her hat. Then a storm of bullets hissed above our heads, tore at leaves, snatched at branches, ricocheted into the darkness.

"Come back!" my father shouted after the young man, but the petrified Lisu ignored him and plunged on down the slope with Ruth. They heard him crashing on through the undergrowth and then nothing more.

In a lull in the gunfire my parents emerged warily into the open. Rough hands grabbed my father and pinioned him against a tree. A man picked up a bamboo rod and whipped it maliciously across his face. There was blood on his cheeks and neck as the hard nodes bit into his flesh. I can only imagine that my mother turned away, instinctively shielding me as well as herself from the sight.

"Why are you beating him?" the brigand chief yelled at my father's tormentor. "Imbecile! Tie his hands. We want him as hostage. He's a good man."

My mother watched as my father was led away. There was nothing she could do. Until the bandits had finished their destruction and looting, there could be no rescue. She hurried back to the house and stood on the balcony waiting for the Christian villagers to return and put out the fires. Ruth was still missing. My mother endured a dreadful night of anxiety, till, at dawn, the young Lisu returned with her frightened daughter. Ruth's dress was torn and stained. Her tears had washed mottled lines in the dirt on her cheeks. Someone had given her a lump of malt toffee and it had become stuck in her thick, black, curly hair.

It had happened before. It could happen again. This was the life Eddie and Bessie had chosen – to serve as missionaries amongst the tribal people of China's Yunnan Province. Taku was their home and this was their life. And now, for a while, it was mine.

My father was away from home for two weeks before he escaped his captors. Typically, he held no grudges for his treatment and found amusement in the direst of occasions.

"One of the bandits had taken your mother's pink nightdress," he told me with some relish many years afterwards. "Looked a pretty picture in it. I told him to take it off – he was embarrassing himself!"

Taku village lies close to the southernmost bend of the Yangtze River, around 8,000 feet above sea level. The region is a crowded system of tightly curving valleys hemmed in by

15

steep-sloped mountains. Here the Eastern Lisu have perched their settlements high above the river ravines on small shelves of land and carved out tiers of terraces for their crops. There was, and still is, no easy route to Taku. It took us a week to walk home from the provincial capital, Yunnanfu (now called Kunming). The narrow, dusty trails wound themselves like thinly defined threads around sheer hillsides above the river valleys, taking us by degrees higher and higher. Only when you came to the crest of the last hill could you see the village across the chasm of one final ravine. As a boy I would stand at the top of this hill and shout as loudly as I could, waiting for the echo to bounce back to me. Then I would plunge down beneath the line of sight and scamper up the opposite slope to the little white church my father had built in 1916.

My father, a young and enterprising single businessman with good prospects, aged twenty-seven, had come to China in October 1906 with the China Inland Mission (CIM), having relinquished his bespoke tailor's business in Oxford. Teachers, preachers and evangelists were needed to work among the ethnic tribes in the south-west. These minority groups were responding to the gospel in great numbers.

Eddie's ministry eventually centred on the Eastern Lisu. At the end of the nineteenth century these people had been locked into a horror of devils, bound in the thrall of animism.

"It was superstitious terror," my father explained to me. "Tangible fear that blighted their every action."

With the arrival of Christian missionaries the Lisu had found salvation in Jesus and now praised God passionately, pouring out their love for God in their love of hymns and harmonies. Across the region my father witnessed the conversion of thousands of tribal folk. In Taku, in the early

1930s, about fifty of the sixty families in the village were Christians. In our church services, many Lisu men and women stood and testified to God's transformation of their lives.

Even as a child I sensed a difference as we travelled from a Christian village to a non-Christian one. I have no recollection of a time when I did not trust in God, nor when prayer and Bible reading were not a natural part of my life. However, I recall one evening when I was about six years old. My father and I were hiking home together, and he had slowed his energetic stride to match my faltering steps. I felt agitated at the sight of the roughly built idol shrines that littered the roadsides. The acute awareness of evil was very real.

"I'm scared," I told him as dusk closed in on us.

He did not indulge my fretting and chided me severely. "Stevie! Satan rules with the dread of demons. God reigns with love. What does Psalm 23 say?"

As we walked on into the nightfall, my hand in his, we recited together, "The Lord is my Shepherd... though I walk through the valley of the shadow of death, I will fear no evil: for thou art with me...",[4] and with each footstep homewards my fears subsided.

Daily life amongst the Lisu was at best basic. The village had no shop. A monthly market had to suffice. There was no gas or electricity. We collected water from a stream in a metal bucket. We grew our own vegetables and there were large fish to be caught in the bigger rivers. Goats' milk and butter were an essential part of our diet. My father received the liver of every animal slaughtered locally because he suffered with sprue. To ensure more time for ministry, my parents hired a male cook and servants to do the household chores. Our mail had to be collected by a courier sent down the mountain to the county town, a day's journey away by pony or on foot.

My father had received basic medical training as preparation for missionary service, and his dispensary and our home were at the far side of the village from the church, distinguished from the plain mud homes of the Lisu by the luxury of whitewashed walls. The mission compound was enclosed within a four-foot-high perimeter wall of dry earth, topped with a parapet of tiles to protect it from the rains. The house itself was relatively large, with four rooms downstairs laid out along a line and a staircase in the middle. Upstairs, the four bedrooms were connected by a long corridor that ran along the back of the house. We had an outside toilet – this was a surprisingly well-built outhouse with a tiled roof. It contained a box with a bucket inside for the adults to sit on, and a matching little box for Ruth and I. The family took baths in a round tin tub in the kitchen.

As a young child I delighted in the freedom I was given. When bandits and brigands didn't threaten, I had generous licence to roam onto the hillsides, to follow a stream to its source, or to sit with Xiao Yang, my Lisu friend, as he tended the family's goats. Set within subtropical conditions, the mountains of Yunnan are rightly known for the beauty of their "perennial spring". There was an abundance of wild lilies, irises and forget-me-nots to be picked. Fields were bright with tall sunflowers and cosmos. And everywhere there was the rich vibrancy of rhododendron bushes. The air was scented with the aroma of wood-smoke and strong, earthy smells. I regularly watched rabbits and spotted monkeys in the thickets, whilst golden pheasants strutted imperiously in and out of the undergrowth, not flustered by my presence. Every night a profound silence, punctuated only by the howl of wolves, held the village in its thraldom, until the dawn freed the birds and insects to sing their songs.

I knew little of life beyond Taku. On very rare occasions we travelled to Kunming; occasionally other missionaries visited us. The fact that every Lisu family stored grain in a coffin appeared conventional to me. As did the fact that each family, except ours, owned a gravestone, kept ready for the unavoidable (a custom they still maintain). Conversely, it did not seem out of place amidst the homespun clothing of the Lisu that my father wore a well-cut suit, a shirt, a tie and a dark grey trilby, and my mother wore blouses, knitted cardigans and skirts. While Xiao Yang wore a flowerpot hat pulled down over his ears, baggy trousers and a smock top with buttons as big as early corn cobs, I was content with V-necked pullovers, short trousers and knee-length socks. There was no concern that I spoke English at home and Lisu with my friends. I readily accepted that Ruth and I were the only children in the village who were not already betrothed in marriage.

I was just three when Ruth left home. She had gone to school, I was told, and I would see her at Christmas. The China Inland Mission boarding school was 2,000 kilometres away as the crow flies, located at Chefoo, a town on the north side of Shandong Province – the distinctive arm of land that points across the Yellow Sea towards Japan. There was no other provision for schooling. At seven years of age Ruth made the journey with my mother, a circuitous route via Hong Kong and Shanghai. The continuum of family life was disrupted and, apart from a few brief months in Australia fifteen years later, we would never again be together for more than a few weeks. In my small world, Ruth had simply disappeared from my domain. After she had gone, all I knew of her adventures and heartaches came from her letters that were hand-carried up those long, dusty trails to Taku.

In August 1934, aged six, it was my turn to start school. I swapped life with my parents, Xiao Yang and the Lisu for a rekindled relationship with Ruth, the roguish camaraderie of boys I had never met and the rigorous conventions of a Western education. My luggage was strapped to the backs of mountain ponies and my father, mother and I walked down to Kunming. Nights were spent in the shelter of coarse, smoke-filled wayside inns. From Kunming we boarded a series of steam-trains that took us to Hanoi in Vietnam and then to Hai Phong, a seaport on the estuary of the Song Hong, the Red River. As a boy brought up in the clasp of great mountain ranges, I was fascinated with the frothing wake of our small steamship to Hong Kong and the ever-changing, fluorescent, crested waves at night. Hong Kong harbour, with its huge liners, cruisers and destroyers, sporting flags from a multitude of countries, was like nothing I had ever seen before.

From Hong Kong to Shanghai we travelled on the *Conte Verde*, a floating Italian castle of extravagance. I enjoyed exploring her countless decks and her labyrinth of corridors and staircases. Even our economy-class cabin seemed a treasure hall in this palace on water.

The fact that my mother and I almost missed the boat added to the adventure! I can still picture my father's anxious face beneath his neatly combed grey hair, as he stood on the lower deck, leaning over the rail. My mother and I hurried along the quay. The ship's siren sounded for departure. The last gangplank was being raised. I was hastily thrust into the hands of a crew member. My mother, then aged forty-three, had to leap across the gap that appeared as the ship moved away from its moorings.

For two days I indulged in huge meals served in a cavern of a dining-room, was captivated by the music of large orchestras and revelled in treats that had never before enchanted my imagination.

In Shanghai I discovered a world where people travelled in taxis, rickshaws, cars and buses. The city seemed akin to a new planet, packed with high-rise buildings requiring lifts and escalators. I thrived on an altogether alien diet, which included heavy clusters of green muscatel grapes and Eskimo pies (an American invention of vanilla ice-cream coated in chocolate and wrapped in tin foil). Even my first trip to a dentist did not diminish my enthusiasm for exploration.

We finally reached Chefoo on a small coastal steamer. The boat sailed past Lighthouse Island into the sheltered waters of the Bluff and threaded a route among the American and British naval vessels stationed in the bay. The school was pointed out to me – a distinctive set of five hefty European buildings standing appropriately erect on the fringe of First Beach. It was an excellent example (as colonial attitudes at the time would have it) of Western civilization, against the backdrop of a range of low Chinese hills. Chefoo was home to a thousand foreigners, served by more than thirty businesses, three banks, the "Chefoo Club", a delicatessen, a German restaurant, six missions, two churches, a newspaper office and an amusement park. Such amenities were not unusual in the Treaty Ports,[5] but Chefoo was unusual in that the foreign residents did not have their territory distinctly marked and had handed the administration of the area over to a Chinese committee.

The siting of the school on an isolated bay in north-east China came by divine circumstance rather than human design. Forced by severe illness to find a place in which to recuperate, the founder of the China Inland Mission, James Hudson Taylor, came to Chefoo in 1879, the year my father was born. A farmer offered to sell Taylor his bean field. He accepted the offer and a convalescence home was constructed from locally quarried stone. Oak beams and Norwegian pine were taken from the *Christian*, a ship which had run aground in the bay. Teak and a host of furniture and fittings were mined from another wreck, the *Ada*. A school was soon established on the site for three children, one of whom, Dr Fred Judd, was our school doctor. By 1894 Chefoo School had grown rapidly to accommodate 200 missionary children.

What I failed to understand on my first day at school was that I would not see my parents again for over a year. Before returning to Taku, they were going to Britain for much-needed recuperation. Both of them were wearied with the ordeals of dengue fever, malaria, typhoid and typhus. My mother moved more slowly due to the onset of osteoarthritis and damage to her upper spine in a riding accident; she had been pulled from her pony by a low-hanging branch. My father, already closer to sixty than fifty, would need to have chunks of flesh cut away from his abdomen to remove an infestation of maggots. Ruth and I returned to Taku at Christmas 1935. We were there for only two weeks before we started the long journey back to school. We enjoyed four of these brief Christmas holidays until 1938, after which the Sino-Japanese War curtailed our travel back to Yunnan. Although my father and mother continued their work in Taku for another twelve years, I was never able to go home to them again.

I knew none of this on the day my parents said their

goodbyes to Ruth and me before climbing into a rickshaw. As they were carried out of sight through the school gates, there was a sense in which they vanished from my life. In time, there came the cruel dawn of understanding – the heart-breaking realization that they would not return in a few days or even a few months. Even their first letters would take weeks to arrive from Britain. It was many years before I ceased to feel that same sorrow of bereavement whenever we separated.

均衡

Kinkou
(Balance)

Boarding-school was an assortment of experiences: some lessons were learned by the hard route, others through carefree diversion. Among my many more enjoyable memories are a catalogue of boyhood escapades – classic boarding-school tales which grow to gallant proportions with time, but which were mainly the innocent or not-quite-so-innocent misdemeanours that groups of boys naturally fall into when left to their own devices.

I shared a dormitory with seven other missionary children. It is difficult to describe (or now to understand) the immense pleasure we got from chucking our slippers at an empty enamel chamber-pot balanced carefully on a chair. Imagine our consternation when, one evening, the heel of a well-aimed slipper went through the bottom of the pot! But our boyish logic easily resolved the dilemma. One boy was away for a few nights. "Shove it under his bed," someone suggested. Several nights later, inevitably, we were woken by the distressed shouts of the lad who had discovered the weakness in our strategy and, more crucially, in his pot!

Neil Yorkston and Brian Thompson were two of my friends at the school. I had known Neil since I was three; we were both born in Kunming. Like me, his father was British and his mother Australian. They were working with the Big

Flowery Miao tribe in the province east of "mine". Brian was the eldest child of an Irish family working in Hebei Province.

As a gang we were not averse to investigating the school drainage system. On one occasion Brian and I crawled into a storm drain (reckoned, in retrospect, to be ten inches wide, eighteen inches high and twenty-five yards in length) beneath the girls' hockey field. He got stuck and I had to shuffle back out. "Wriggle," I told him. "Wriggle harder!" I extricated him from his plight by pulling at his legs.

This should have been a lesson in itself, but we had not finished our foolery for that particular afternoon. We surfaced from the drainage ditch and raced up to the centre of the pitch in search of the other end of the pipe. Brian, Neil and I prised off the circular concrete lid.

"You can get through that," said Brian confidently. He was bigger than me and he had got trapped last time. Clearly, I needed to prove I could get trapped too. Which I duly did, some feet along the drain. I had pushed on around a gentle bend in the pipe and could see light at the end of the tunnel, when it became obvious that I was going no further.

"I'm stuck."

There was no response.

"I'm stuck!" I yelled.

There was still no response. My muffled voice was not carrying back up the pipe. I began to panic. With my arms stretched out ahead of me, I had little leverage. I pushed backwards, but my body was wedged in place. I needed to take my own advice. I wriggled for all I was worth. It seemed to be an eternity before I emerged and sat shakily on the grass.

Seeing Brian's bottom in the air and his head down a drain, a group of younger boys had gathered. They all greatly admired my exploits, but it still gives me nightmares to this day!

On another unwise occasion, one winter, seven of us were allowed out on a hike. We headed for a local hill on which stood a small pagoda. Finding crude cracks chiselled out in its walls, we helped each other up a risky climb of fifteen feet. The view, such as it was, quickly lost its appeal as a fierce and bitter wind threatened to blow us off the ledge around the wall. Frightened of losing grip on the icy holds, five boys became captives in our "castle" while I and another friend made it to safety. A sound piece of advice was yelled after us as we began the three-mile walk back to school: "Bring the toilet ladder!"

This excellent solution proved not to be an option. The ladder, used to climb up to fix the plumbing, was missing. Instead of struggling several miles across frozen tracts of land with a ladder, I had to struggle to keep up with a burly and irritated schoolmaster, who carried a long rope and a nice line on "miserable offenders". His irritation was not eased by the discovery that the five captives had already been sprung from their keep by a Chinese farmer with the aid of a rake. My nine-mile act of "heroism" was rewarded with having to write a 200-word essay on "How to avoid doing foolhardy things".

Others had a more alarming encounter. In January 1935 seventy pupils and five staff, returning from their Christmas break, had boarded the *Tungchow* at Shanghai and apparently sailed off into thin air. Pirates had seized the ship, killing the commander of the Russian guards charged with the boat's protection. White stripes were painted around the funnel and the vessel was renamed. The incident was headlined across the world.

It was four days before a British aircraft spotted the ship parked in Bias Bay, a regular pirates' lair, near Hong Kong. The hijackers fled with money and jewels they had fleeced from the passengers, and $250,000 in what proved to be worthless banknotes, because they lacked official signatures.

At school, the rescued Chefusians regaled us with tales of dodging bullets and showed us pieces of cloth they extravagantly claimed they had pinched from the pirates. A grey jersey with holes at the elbows – a pirate's pullover – was placed in a glass display case as a prime exhibit of their adventure. The hostages were definitely in the class of heroes. But, more heroically to me, they had missed a whole ten days of lessons!

As we grew older our interests, of course, matured. Girls, in particular, changed from unavoidable classmates to attractions. One of my friends, Lance, inadvertently got me into trouble over a girl he became infatuated with. When I was around fourteen I set myself up as an amateur photographer and sold my pictures to other pupils. Lance was keen to get snaps of Mary. Enterprisingly, I plonked myself in front of her at a tennis match and by reversing the camera took several photographs of her.

Eager to make a quick dollar or two with my pictures of the tennis, I cycled to the Chinese photographers and asked for the photos to be developed as rapidly as possible. Unfortunately, the shop manager gave them to a senior boy to deliver, and he had no aversion to flicking through the pile before handing them over. It did not take long for the boys' dorms to be buzzing with the news that Steve Metcalf had a crush on Mary. And it wasn't long before Mary's uncle came demanding to see the photos.

"It was a mistake," I stuttered. "They weren't good. I... got rid of them."

This was closer to a lie than a half-truth. I had given them to Lance, as arranged. To Lance's chagrin it also transpired that his "beloved" now had her sights on me. Through a friend she hinted that she would like the negatives, wanted my picture and suggested meeting. Nothing came of it!

At school the essential truths of Christianity were taught and the practices were mandatory. On Sundays Ruth and I joined the crocodile of a hundred or so children being marched a mile along the seafront, past the rank of European hotels, to Consulate Hill on the edge of town. We were apparently nonconformists, since we joined the procession to the Union Church. St Andrews was for the Anglicans – a detail I accepted without comprehension. We learned little from the adult-orientated services but at least the walk helped to maintain my relationship with Ruth.

We were encouraged to find time to pray on our own. Morning and evening prayers were conducted by a rota of schoolmasters. Ironically, the only message that sticks with me was delivered by one of the stuffier members of staff with a pedantic style of repetition.

"If you are walking in the light, you are not walking in the darkness, are you?"

"No!"

"If you are walking in the darkness, you are not walking in the light, are you?

"No!"

Far more enlightening were the non-compulsory and fun events, such as the Children's Special Service Missions on the beach each summer, complete with a sand pulpit and bucketfuls of activities.

It was music, however, that opened a door for my personal experience of God. The singing of the Eastern Lisu had always stirred me. Our services at the little white church resonated with powerful worship, glorying God in harmonies that literally rang down the valley. Now I discovered other forms of lyrics and tunes that were equally compelling. As a member of the school choir I responded to the words of new hymns such as "Facing a task unfinished that drives us to our knees" and "Thou who wast rich beyond all splendour, all for love's sake becamest poor".[6] I was captivated by lines from a performance of Stainer's *Crucifixion*: "Could ye not watch with me one brief hour?"[7] It may come as little surprise, therefore, to learn that my commitment to Christ eventually came about through music – the result of a few stolen notes played on a harmonica I filched from a friend!

My school reports gently revealed the reality about my academic prowess: "He is very good on the whole." I now appreciate the subtle tone which allowed my parents to read between the lines. At the time, I was not sure which "hole" was being referred to. My mind was generally elsewhere in lessons. Often exploring the hillside above Taku. Frequently wondering what my parents were doing. I wanted to see my father pulling the teeth of a patient. Or watch him in the dispensary measuring out medicine from bottles of aspirin, castor oil and quinine, and handing out tins of Epsom salts and Mecca ointment (an antiseptic cream). I wanted to be at home with my mother. I wanted to speak Lisu with Xiao Yang. Or wander down through the village where the women, some dressed in their intricately embroidered tunics and skirts, would expertly crack open sunflower seeds for me with their teeth. And I wanted to be in our little white church, listening to the swell of Lisu voices in worship. In truth, despite my school friendships, I often felt lonely.

If my confidence was lacking in the classroom, it was bolstered by the knowledge that I could hold my own on the sports field. The school, blessed with the ethos of a British system and the motivation of Victorian achievement, encouraged excellence in sport as well as academic attainment. Our headmaster, Patrick A. Bruce (known as "Pa" Bruce), had played cricket for Cambridge and rugby at Harlequins. Monday, Wednesday and Friday sessions were designated for "serious" sport and there were compulsory daily plunges into the cold water of Chefoo Bay.

I captained the football team and enjoyed gymnastics, rowing and swimming. I was less accomplished at cricket and retreated behind the stumps as wicket-keeper. It was my ability at running that later brought me the friendship of Eric Liddell, gold and bronze Olympic medallist in Paris in 1924. Eric had held his head high on the great running tracks of Europe, but he was also a quiet, humble man of God. He, more than most, taught me to love the Japanese.

窮地

Kyuchi
(Straits)

My only contact with Taku was the letters that arrived from my parents. They devotedly wrote each week; one writing to Ruth, the other to me. In our twenty-five-minute lunch breaks we sat together on the school steps to swap the latest news and share our secrets. Of the two, my mother was the more imaginative writer, describing life in Taku in animated detail over four, five or six pages of the clear handwriting she maintained till the week she died. These letters fed my thirst for contact with life amongst the Lisu that I missed so much. But, despite the faithfulness in their writing, arrival was frequently delayed or disrupted. The postal route from Yunnan was convoluted. The onset of the Sino-Japanese war in the summer of 1937 brought additional havoc to the service. And, beyond that, there was coming a time when the service would fail altogether.

I had been at Chefoo three years when the Japanese invasion of North China brought a sea change which would ultimately result in the closure of the school.[8] I remember running the last half-mile of the school cross-country run, anxious to secure second place, sprinting past knots of armed Japanese soldiers wearing khaki tunics, knee-length boots and steel helmets, some with swords dangling from their waists. It had taken some months for the occupying army to turn its attention to Chefoo, but they were now strengthening their grip on Shandong Province. Fortunately, there was no battle over the town; rich Chinese businessmen bribed the local government troops to retreat. For the foreign population the occupation was something of a relief. The war had created a power vacuum and, while Chefoo had escaped the worst of the turmoil, serious riots and looting had been reported in other Treaty Ports.

At first, the Japanese proved to be charitable, careful not to encroach onto the property and freedoms of the foreign community. A leaflet, written in Chinese, was dropped from the sky. Under the title "The New Order in East Asia", it declared that "The Japanese Army is an army of strict discipline, protecting good citizens... business will prosper once more." At school we were rarely troubled, though we were acutely aware of the bitter conflict between Japanese and Chinese. School friends from Manchuria and other occupied areas returned to Chefoo from their homes with news of the imprisonment of Chinese church pastors, atrocious tales of massacres and horrific details of torture inflicted by Japanese hands. One man I met years afterwards spoke of the Japanese as a "killing machine" and of their "lust" for conquest. He was forced to learn Japanese and worship the Emperor. Four CIM nurses, who fled the fighting, related having to treat appalling bayonet and sword wounds. A mother from a Nanjing mission hospital had treated a Chinese woman whose flesh had been ripped into shreds by war-crazed soldiers. I found myself torn with anger at the dreadful stories I heard. Yet, confusingly, the Japanese who served in the local shops we frequented were kind adults. It was only later I discovered that they were forced to spy on us by the brutal *Kempeitai*,

Japan's "Gestapo" – their uniformed military police.

In 1939, as Europe tipped over the brink of conciliation into war, our situation deteriorated. The Japanese grew more confident of their rule in China and Westerners found themselves increasingly isolated. Permission for foreigners to travel across the borders into Free China was hard to secure. Ruth and I could not return home for Christmas.

In Chefoo, with no clear boundaries to mark colonial territory, the doorstep of their property became the threshold over which expats stepped into Japanese imperialism. Where once politeness and civility had been a veneer to Japanese ambition, now the posturing was exposed. The Americans were advised to leave, and many did. We watched Japanese seaplanes being loaded with bombs in the bay. Bank accounts were frozen. Post in and out of the town was no longer delivered. Anti-British demonstrations were forced on the town's Chinese population.

On 2 May 1940 our local staff, among them the rotund laundry-man we called "Zerubbabel", the lean, melancholy "Priest" and the burly "Pirate Bill", walked off campus on strike. According to one of the staff, we children worked with "relish" to maintain the school until the strike was called off with equal suddenness thirty hours later.

Germany's defeat of first Holland and then France, left swathes of colonial empire exposed. A year later Japan reached agreement with the French to annexe Indo-China and poured 40,000 troops into Saigon to consolidate its claims on South China. Britain and the USA declared "economic" war on Japan. The Japanese did not back down. In December 1941 Japanese bombers appeared over Pearl Harbour and, in a pre-emptive strike on the US navy, unleashed warfare in the

Pacific. We were no longer neutrals in the struggle between China and Japan. Japanese schoolboys, sons of merchants in the town, threw both insults and stones over the school wall. We were now the enemy.

Earlier in 1941 Ruth had completed her schooling, and it was decided she should go to Australia to live with a family friend while training as a nurse. From Chefoo she and one of her friends, Betty, made their way to Manila, where they were caught up in the conflict. When the Japanese attacked the Philippines on the afternoon of 8 December, Ruth and Betty escaped on the last ship out of Manila Harbour. My mother, who came to Chefoo to help Ruth pack, not foreseeing what was to happen, had made her way back to my father in Taku without me. At fourteen, I was suddenly and utterly cut off from my family.

At the school we were crudely roused to the reality of our status by the arrival of a dozen soldiers demanding the arrest of our headmaster, Pa Bruce. He was confined with other foreign men in the Astor House Hotel, where he was interrogated by the *Kempeitai* as a spy. They released him as a goodwill gesture for Christmas morning, and then detained him again until 25 January. He was fortunate to return. Bob McMullan, head of a Chefoo trading company, was hauled off to the provincial capital, his fate unknown till April, when news of his death was callously conveyed to his widow. His jailers had, it was rumoured, slowly and painfully poisoned him.

Our compound became the property of the "Imperial Japanese Army", a fact underlined by a notice posted on the school gates and the intimidating presence of soldiers holding rifles extended with fixed bayonets. Outside the school gates I was required to carry my identity card and forced to wear a white armband, four inches wide, stamped with a black "B" for "British". Inexorably the Japanese commandeered more of our buildings, squeezing staff and pupils into ever-tighter spaces. We lacked sufficient Chinese staff and finance. Food was rationed.

We were shocked at an order that all the senior girls be recruited as prostitutes for the use of the Japanese Navy. Pa Bruce emphatically rejected the demands. The Japanese, maintaining "face",[9] decided to defer the matter. There was, however, little rejoicing over this "victory". Other girls, Chinese and Korean, would be commandeered into service instead.

The school closed its high metal double-leaf gates on 5 November 1942. Of the 320 boarders present when the Pacific War started, 120 remained, the rest having returned to their parents. We were ordered to vacate the premises and move to a "civilian assembly centre". Under the surveillance of soldiers in olive-green uniforms, one of our teachers, Stanley Houghton, led the boys up the road, singing "God is still on the throne",[10] to Temple Hill, a former American Presbyterian mission compound.

Before we left Chefoo School I carried a bundle of my parents' letters (about 350 of them in total) out onto the school playing field. They seemed an additional burden, taking up room in my packing that could be given to more "important" items. I shuffled the flimsy pages into a pile and lit a match. The heat of the tiny flame traced brown lines along the seared edge of the first sheet. The writing seemed to grow in intensity, and the black ink was strangely illuminated for a few seconds before the paper darkened and disintegrated. I stood back and watched until the whole pile had been reduced to meaningless ashes. Now, of course, I regret my detached pragmatism. These were letters that told stories that I have long since forgotten, that chronicled the lives of Eastern Lisu Christians, that expressed deeper emotions than the contents divulged.

鳥籠

Torikago
(Caged Bird)

Behind the stone-wall and barbed-wire confines of the school
on Temple Hill lay a church, a hospital, teaching blocks and
several large, detached family houses previously occupied
and trashed by the Japanese army. Three sections had been
marked out: one for the hundred or so members of the
business community who had remained in Chefoo; another
for the female section of the school; and a third for males. The
three houses designated for the Chefoo boys stood in a row
like sentries, each one surrounded by a low wall. Thirteen of
us, aged fifteen and sixteen, were jammed into an attic room.
The girls, in a house 400 yards away, were even more cramped
than us.

Any privileges of colonial life we had clung to were
removed. The Chinese staff needed to run the school did not
come with us. Everything had to be done by ourselves or
not at all. We had to clean and cook, sweep floors, cut wood
and shovel coal to keep the boiler hot, do the laundry, grind
corn, peel potatoes and vegetables. Among other tasks, I
was assigned to boil up oatmeal for breakfast, putting it in a
padded box to allow it to cook slowly overnight.

Once a semblance of order had been established, the
teachers, being teachers, were not slow to restart classes.
Structure, they stated, would maintain morale and divert our

minds from the hardships ahead.

However, our conditions eventually took their toll. I went down with, first, Hepatitis A and then a raging fever. My temperature racked upwards over several days until sulpha drugs were obtained from the town's hospital. The cure was effective, but I was left weak – and bored – lying on my bed in the attic.

John, a year older than me and going on six foot two compared to my diminutive five foot five, occupied the bed next to me. Some weeks earlier he had ripped into me for playing his harmonica. "You're not to touch it," he had insisted fiercely, grabbing it back off me.

His "selfishness" had irritated me. I could play the harmonica and had lost mine. He, on the other hand, couldn't knock out any sort of tune. Perhaps if I had known he had TB and was trying to protect me, things would have been different. But I didn't, and the urge to please myself was strong.

The instrument lay in its box, pristine and an arm's length away. Everyone else was in lessons. I dug out the instrument from amongst John's few possessions. My audacity gave me no pleasure. Having warbled out a few tunes, I returned the instrument to its place. Guilt burst a dam of grief inside me. I choked on my sobbing as the tears ran unhindered down my cheeks and soaked wet patches onto my pyjamas. There was no way to stop it.

It was one of the most extraordinary moments of my life. Such a small thing, with such eternal consequences. I cried to God for forgiveness. A fresh emotion welled up within me. I was drenched in a joy I had never experienced before. I felt a peace that filled every part of me. I responded to God's grace with song after song of thanksgiving until I finally slid softly into sleep.

When I awoke, one of my friends, Stan, was standing over my bed. "You OK?" he asked.

"I'm fine! Just fine!" I grinned with the elation of it all. "God has healed me. He's forgiven my sins."

Stan looked at me awkwardly. Clearly, my reply had not been what he expected!

There was a gentle irony in all this. My reconciliation with God, the "treaty" I needed more than any other, coincided with a declaration of human hostilities in which I was the enemy and in which I had been reduced to a powerless prisoner of war. I was not the only one in the camp to respond to Christ at this time. My spiritual freedom, and that of others, was, I believe, God's response to the anguish of missionary parents and mission supporters. Shock-waves must have rippled out from China with the news of the school's internment. Prayer was their only possible response.

There seemed to be a surge of spirituality all around us. I was suddenly hungry to read all I could about famous Christians and scavenged for books from the meagre library that the school staff had salvaged. I worked my way through the biographies of William Booth in Britain, Adoniram Judson of Burma, Dwight L. Moody from the USA and others. I lost myself in the basement as often as duties allowed, sitting amongst a heap of bags and furniture, poring over each book, coveting time spent alone in prayer and Bible study. I began to write my own commentary on the Bible verses I read. I worked through Mark, then Philippians and moved on to Job and Esther. I had no doubt that the Holy Spirit was at work in igniting this unquenchable desire for God's blessing.

The camp at Temple Hill ultimately proved to be impracticable. In a population of around 400, approximately a third were classed as minors. The burden on the active adult population in caring for children and the elderly proved too great.

The pleasant warmth of autumn soon descended into the severe chill of winter. It was not unknown for the bay to freeze over, the foam on the sea collecting in icy mounds four or five feet high that floated like boats on the waves. In contrast, the dry winds of the short spring were hot and harsh. Summer was humid and broke in September into typhoon storms of lashing rain.

As our money ran out, we could no longer buy additional provisions from the Chinese. Meat, butter, sugar and flour were in short supply. A diet of bean curd, coarse millet bread and cabbage was more often than not the only food on offer. Clothing was outgrown or reduced to rags. There was illness and mental breakdown. Our attempts at routine and civility were under persistent strain.

We posed no threat to the Japanese, but we were becoming a liability. We were informed that we would be moved to a larger internment camp, a hundred miles away at Weifang. The first part of our journey would be by boat to Qingdao and then inland by train.

The wartime brutality of the Japanese is well recorded. But those who showed genuine sympathy for their captives need also to be remembered. Major Kosaka, the Temple Hill camp commandant, made our lives a little better by his kindness. When I was ill, he visited me and went to the local hospital with our doctor to obtain the best medicine. And when it was time to move, he travelled to the new camp himself and, having seen the conditions, advised us to take everything we possibly could, including our beds and mattresses. I recall him standing at the end of the railway platform at Qingdao, saluting while the whole length of our train pulled out of the station. No doubt it was protocol, as he handed over responsibility for us to new guards, but his bearing carried with it a mark of respect for the men, women and children who had been under his care.

In September 1943 army trucks drove into our camp. We were bundled into them and trundled down to the harbour – our progress watched by itinerant crockery menders and cobblers, by a miscellany of merchants, by barbers, calligraphers, fortune-tellers, wood-carvers, street-dentists and ear-cleaners. I had little left of any value. I had sold my collection of over 3,000 stamps and bought saccharine with the money. The few possessions that I counted important I carried in an old metal locker-box. As we left the harbour, a small launch pulled alongside. Our Chefoo baker was making his last delivery of bread.

The boat was over-burdened with passengers and rats. Despite the bread delivery, there was a lack of food. We slept, huddled together in long lines, on bare boards down in the hold. The atmosphere was stifling and the smells from poor plumbing were nauseating. We feared the early autumn storms and American submarines. Weifang, our destination, was two days away by our roundabout boat-and-train route. We were to be interned in another American Presbyterian mission compound – a larger prison with gates that carried the now inappropriate title, "Le Dao Yuan" – The Courtyard of the Happy Way.

継走

Keisou
(Relay Race)

Weifang Civilian Internment Centre was located about three miles from the railway station. Our party was again jammed into trucks and carted on a forty-minute grind along the cobbled streets of the town, through the large gates in its old walls and out into the countryside. The landscape looked lifeless – flat farming land, largely denuded of trees. Our final destination had all the demeanour of an archetypal prison: institutionalized brick buildings standing out above six-foot-high walls, guarded by electric fences. Japanese soldiers poked machine-guns in our direction from stubby circular turrets, which squatted beneath wooden Chinese coolie-hat roofs at intervals along the compound walls.

We arrived around 5 p.m., a column of unkempt refugees, clinging to our few possessions, dragging the heavier loads through the stinking mud of the makeshift roads that ran the length of the camp. We were not the first internees. There were hundreds of men, women and children lining the streets, standing at doorways, leaning out of grey-paned windows, all watching our laboured progress. The drabness of their dirty attire and the weary dullness of their expressions aped our own dishevelled fatigue.

It was understandable that a ragbag of young children and old folk was not a welcome sight for them, but they made us cups of weak tea, lacking milk and sugar, and members of the camp's Quarters Committee pointed us to our sleeping berths. I was allotted a place in the cramped confines of a dormitory made up in the classroom of a former teaching block. This was one of the largest buildings, complete with stylish balconies, arched colonnades and a lofty square bell-tower.[11]

Later I moved to "Shadyside" Hospital, where I shared an attic room with seven others. There we enjoyed the comfort of views beyond the compound walls, where thin Chinese farmers and their families ploughed fields by hand, irrigated and harvested crops. Their lives evoked a degree of normality denied to us.

Our arrival came after the repatriation of around 200 Americans, and this was followed by the departure of a large contingent of Roman Catholic priests and nuns headed for Beijing – 400 Dutch and Belgians, whom papal delegations to Tokyo claimed to be citizens of the Vatican and therefore neutrals in the war. The priests and nuns had been able and enterprising members of the community and were sorely missed. We must have appeared a poor substitute, but at least there was a little more room for everyone. At its peak the camp had numbered around 2,000. When we arrived there were fewer than 1,500 internees, until the surprising arrival in December of 100 Italians, who were housed in the unimaginatively named "Italian Quarter".

We were a cosmopolitan lot. There were around 1,000 British and 200 Americans. There were Canadians, Greeks, Norwegians, South Africans, and sixty Russian women (married to Westerners) and their children – all sharing space with a collection of Cubans, Filipinos, Hawaiians, Iranians,

Palestinian Jews, Panamanians, Parsees and Uruguayans. Influential businessmen found themselves in the company of bankrupts, shopkeepers lived alongside thieves, lawyers rubbed along with men more used to propping up bars, and single lady missionaries slept in dorms with former prostitutes. Roughly a quarter of this strange community were aged over sixty and a similar number were less than fifteen years of age.

Together we made up a hapless miscellany of humanity dealing with the deprivations of detention and loss of privacy, coping with the choice aromas of inadequate washing and toilet facilities, battling with plagues of vermin – bedbugs, flies, mosquitoes, rats – and facing the daily struggle to feed ourselves adequately; all within the confines of an L-shaped area 200 yards long and measuring, at its widest, 150 yards.

We were fortunate to have arrived at Weifang after the commencement of internment. Like Temple Hill, this well-equipped compound had been trashed. For the first groups of internees there had been an uncomfortable period of establishing order amidst the chaos. The kitchen, medical, shower and toilet blocks had been reduced to little more than empty shells. Broken benches, chairs, desks, tables and metal fittings lay in ruined heaps in the open. Ordered by the Japanese to arrange their own affairs, this conglomerate of nations and know-how embarked on debate over how to organize themselves. What emerged was a skeleton of civilized life – nine committees with uncertain jurisdiction over discipline, engineering, education, finance, general affairs, labour, medicine, quarters and supplies, backed by a degree of compliance in the majority to keep selfish anarchy at bay.

The camp predominantly comprised single-storey

terraces of basic rooms, with a few substantial dormitory blocks, an assembly hall and a hospital. The site was blessed with a good number of trees and, here and there, care had been taken to plant out beds of vegetables. Personal touches to living quarters helped to counter the austerity of cheek-by-jowl living.

The central track that ran the length of the site had been named Main Street, with a parallel thoroughfare called Tin-Pin Alley. Side "roads" had been given outlandish names such as Sunset Boulevard, Old Kent Road, Peitaiho Beach, Wall Street and Leek Avenue. We even had our own short version of a Lovers' Lane, but I had little interest in finding a girlfriend, let alone a regular niche along its fairly crowded length.

Our lives, under a rigorous combination of the camp's committees and the Chefoo School regime, were quickly structured into communal labour teams and a continuation of our education. I was, at fifteen, now one of the older boys and was assigned to a Chefoo contingent to pump water, a job previously done by the Catholic priests. Half-hour shifts entailed swinging on a three-foot metal handle, coercing water from a well into one of four forty-gallon drums around the site. These mini water-towers stood on stands supported by four large round poles, ten to fifteen feet above the ground. We manned the pumps from six in the morning until around nine at night; otherwise the water in the tanks would run out.

School was conducted on long wooden benches in our dorms, with a small arm-rest on which to put textbooks or on which to lean as we wrote. Books were in very short supply and our teachers worked exceedingly hard to keep us on track for the Oxford Matriculation exams they devised for us. True to form, I did not excel. I did well enough in Biology, English

Literature, General Science and Scripture but managed only a pass in English Language and French. This secured me the curious overall result of a "Pass – Compensated"!

From the pump teams I was quickly moved on to work in one of the two kitchens, each required to feed between 700 and 800 people every day. A shift of six internees was designated for work, one day in three, starting at 6 a.m. and calling a halt at 7 p.m. My team, under the direction of a congenial American, were an eclectic bunch: a French Canadian businessman, a White Russian company security officer, a Belgian priest and a Canadian who had worked with British-American Tobacco.

We cooked in large shallow woks and ate out of tin cans. Heat was coaxed from briquettes of black coal-dust mixed with handfuls of mud, which we scraped from the dirt of the compound. Working in the kitchens had its advantages. There were days when there was simply not enough food to go round and internees were turned away from the canteens. As kitchen staff, we were able to supplement our meagre diet with titbits and scraps of food.

Carts carrying the day's provisions were driven into the compound each morning. We were given millet, soya and other types of beans, and sorghum, a reddish-brown cereal crop the Chinese used mainly for chicken feed. The sorghum was boiled until something akin to a tasteless chocolate pudding filled our pots. If it was not ground up in advance, forty-eight hours of boiling were needed to produce something edible.

Inadequate amounts of meat appeared from time to time. These less-than-inviting slabs of sometimes indeterminate flesh were boiled up immediately, before they went rotten. The internees had built their own bakery, and flour for bread and cake was ground from adulterated wheat on millstones.

In the early months vegetables arrived in good quantities. We devised a multitude of ways to make "menus" seem varied. Great heaps of cucumbers proved a particular problem. We served them in all manner of guises. We sautéed, steamed and stewed them. We ate them raw. They gave us diarrhoea. Years later I discovered that the Japanese salted them down as pickles. At other times sweet potatoes were plentiful and people fermented the skins to produce an alcoholic drink. Chinese tea leaves were done to death to extract the last dregs of flavour.

*

"Here, Steve."

The trim, balding, middle-aged Scotsman at my side gently pushed a pair of running shoes into my hands.

"Your shoes look past repair," he added. "These may last you a few weeks."

It was the winter of 1944/45. In the warmer weather I ran around without shoes, but sub-zero temperatures were no place for bare feet. Any extra scrap of threadbare clothing was a godsend. There was little attractive about the shoes I was being offered. Patched up and sewn with string, they could only be described as dilapidated. I should have realized they meant a lot to my benefactor and guessed that he had spent time and effort working on them – for me. But he was a quiet, diffident man and I had frozen feet.

Eric Henry Liddell, the "Flying Scotsman", was born in January 1902 in Tianjin, north-west China, the son of London Missionary Society parents. His phenomenal prowess on the rugby field as a Scottish international and on the athletics track had made him a celebrity in Britain. But, in summer 1925, he had returned to China and served first as a science teacher at the Tianjin Anglo-Chinese School and then at the rural mission station in Hebei Province, where he had lived as a child. Now he was interned with us at Weifang, separated from his wife and three daughters who were in Canada.

I had met Eric on my first Sunday in camp. He led our Bible Class, taking his texts from the Sermon on the Mount. His enthusiasm for his subject and his winsome manner immediately drew me to him. As the days, weeks and months passed, I began to understand that here was a Christian man who not only loved these passages of Scripture but lived them out, whatever his circumstances. He became a significant role model, not only to me, but to dozens of teenagers and children who benefited from the sports and educational activities he organized on their behalf.

I remember a hard-fought relay race. As I received the baton, my rival for first place was already into his stride. I pounded after him, aware that Eric, coach for the opposing team, was standing beyond the finishing tape. I chased on, taking inches, then feet out of the advantage. With just yards to go, I burst into the lead, breasting the tape as winner. Exhausted, I collapsed into Eric's arms, while Eric, even though his team had lost, exulted in my hard-fought victory. It was typical of the man – magnanimous in defeat, euphoric in the manner of the win.

My ability at all sorts of sports – athletics, softball, football, gymnastics and touch rugby – gave me greater contact with Eric. He offered me advice on running and asked me to join his Recreation Committee. I enjoyed the leadership role; I found it brought me the respect of those around me and bolstered my self-confidence. Much as I would have sat for hours listening to him, Eric's modesty meant he rarely talked about his own achievements. He did, however, impart the greatest challenge to my life – "You should pray for the Japanese."

Was it really possible to pray for the men who had incarcerated us in this wretched prison and stood guard over us with guns? For jailers who kept me apart from my family?

夜明け
Yoake
(Daybreak)

For the most part, I lived in ambivalence about the guards who had locked us behind the compound walls. By and large they kept their inscrutable distance. They lived in better, more spacious quarters on the south side of the site, an area out of bounds to the internees and previously the residence of the American missionaries. The guards could not speak English and few of us had any Japanese. Sadly, they were thoroughly indoctrinated with an arrogant rhetoric of national superiority and hatred of their enemies, particularly the Chinese.

We maintained reasonable order. While there were minor victories in "getting one over on the Japs", we were not eager to test their patience. Escape held little attraction. As civilians, unlike military personnel, we were under no duty to evade capture. It was perhaps 600 miles across Japanese-occupied territory into Free China. There were no guarantees that the local Chinese would not hand us over for profit. The ongoing civil conflict between the Chinese Nationalist and Communist armies did not necessarily make freedom from the Japanese a safer option.

We were required to attend a daily roll call. Divided into sections, we would congregate on open spaces, passing the time as best we could until the guards were satisfied with the count. I was *ni-ju-san* – number twenty-three. We were not above having a joke at the guards' expense. In turn we counted off:

"Itchy" ("one" in Japanese being *ichi*).

"Knee" ("two" was *ni*).

"Catchy."

"Flea."

Any disruption to the count meant we had to start again. As a consequence, the daily totals chalked up on a blackboard in the guardroom sometimes varied by a wide margin![12]

For the rest of the time we preferred not to be alone when approached by the guards. Evenings were particularly difficult, with a curfew in place. The toilet blocks stood some distance away from our living quarters and German Shepherd dogs prowled the grounds. There was the amusing story of one unfortunate internee who, caught by a guard with his dog between the toilet block and the dorm, could only remember that the Japanese for "toilet" was similar to the English word for a musical instrument. "Violin! Trumpet! Drum!" he yelled, until finally he stumbled upon the correct word – "Banjo!" – our nearest equivalent to *benjo*.

Our biggest problems stemmed from the black market. Shortages of food and a willingness among the Chinese to risk life and limb to trade with the foreigners opened up a Pandora's box of schemes and ploys to channel goods into the compound. Eggs were rolled through holes in the walls, cabbages and live chickens were flung over the electric fence.

One day I was with a younger boy who had a Japanese mother and spoke the language well. He deftly lifted an egg from a basket being carried into the Japanese quarters. When one of the duty guards engaged him briefly in conversation, he became so nervous that the egg slipped from his hand and splattered down onto his bare feet. The guard, oblivious to how the boy had got the egg in the first place, roared with laughter at his plight.

While much of this black-market activity passed off undetected, it was not without cost. Westerners caught in the act spent a week or two in solitary confinement. The sight of a Chinese man hung up on the electric fence, left as a warning to others, was an horrific reminder of the consequences of getting caught.

Matthew 5:43 says, "Love your enemies". Was it really possible to pray for the Japanese? Our Bible study discussions had led us to think of this as an ideal, not a practical reality. Eric Liddell pulled us back to his theme:

"Matthew five includes the words, 'Pray for those who persecute you.' We spend time praying for the people we love, the people we like. But Jesus told us to pray for those we don't like.

"When you hate, you are self-centred. When you pray, you are God-centred. Praying changes your attitude. It is hard to hate those you pray for."

Eric died from a brain tumour on 21 February 1945, aged forty-three, three weeks after he had given me his running shoes. Internees packed out the church for the funeral service on the following Saturday. I wore his shoes and helped to carry his coffin. The cemetery lay within the Japanese quarters and only a few of us were allowed, under guard, to the graveside. As we shivered in the desperate cold, chilled by a freezing wind, we lowered the coffin into the ground and listened to the Beatitudes being read. We boys had lost our champion; our community had lost one of its real saints. I felt crushed by the moment. His family would not even know he had died. The final resting-place of this renowned athlete was an obscure corner of a foul prison camp, marked by a crude cross with his name written on it in shoe-blacking.

"Is this all?" I asked myself. "Is this all that happens to such a great man?" There seemed a futility in his death that belied his contribution to life.

Between us, we picked up the jobs Eric had left behind. There at the graveside I also picked up the baton he had held – the baton of forgiveness. I told God that if I made it out of the camp alive, I would go to Japan as a missionary.

People have asked me what happened to those running shoes and whether I ever raced against Eric. We raced twice. On the first occasion, as one of a team of earnest teenagers, I lined up some yards ahead of him. I was bent on beating our Olympic hero, a man who had held a world record for four years. God made him fast, but that day I stayed ahead of him. On the second occasion the course was longer and even though he was in his early forties, I was no match for his speed. As for the running shoes, they barely lasted out the winter. I should perhaps have kept them. But I gladly exchanged them for a pair of US Army boots.

It was also in this camp, six months earlier, that I had said a sad farewell to Brian Thompson, my daredevil confederate in our exploits at Chefoo. We were out at Assembly Point Six – our basketball ground by the hospital – for the 7 p.m. roll call. Brian and Neil Yorkston had just surfaced from a Hebrew lesson. We shuffled into our allotted positions amongst the 241 internees strung out along makeshift lines – a bunch of teenagers resigned to yet another needless counting of heads. It was a languid August evening, steeped in high humidity. Neil stifled a yawn and stretched his arms above his head, brushing against one of the unsheathed wires that hung in lazy catenaries across the playing field. These cables supplied electricity for the street lighting from sundown to 10 p.m. Recent rains had softened the ground around the poles that supported the power lines, causing the wires to hang lower than normal.

"It's live!" Neil drew his hand away sharply.

Another of our group, Henry, reached up. "Yes…"

Brian stretched his right arm upwards to another wire. He was barefoot. The ground was damp. His fingers curled around the strand. A loud gasp escaped his lips. We watched in helplessness as he fell, his head thumping against the ground, dragging the cable down with him. He was sixteen. The doctor said he was dead before some of the adults were able to knock the wire out of his hands with a wooden deckchair. The Japanese called it suicide.[13]

*

The Japanese were convinced we had a wireless, as we were somehow keeping abreast of news of the war. In the last year of our internment, a "Rumour of the Day" began to appear on the Bulletin Board. Its accuracy made our captors suspicious, but they never found our radio. It was, in fact, outside the camp, hidden in the hills.

In June 1944 Arthur Hummel, an American teacher,[14] and Laurie Tipton, a British employee of the British-American Tobacco Company, slipped through the compound defences and joined the Chinese Resistance. This security lapse threw the Japanese into a fit of reprisal; thankfully, it resulted only in the instigation of a second roll call each day and changes in our accommodation.

Hummel and Tipton organized ways of getting news into the compound. Written on a strip of silk stuffed up the nose of a coolie, a message could be deposited in the gutter when the man cleared his sinuses – an action that, while unappealing to a Westerner, was normal for the Chinese.

Other news was gleaned from the careful reading of Japanese propaganda. Whilst every victory was jubilantly reported, it became clear that the war was being waged closer and closer to the shores of Japan.

In May 1945, when a little note on the Bulletin Board announced that the German army had capitulated and the war in Europe was over, our hopes of release rose just a little. Any delight had to be tempered by our plight. As the Allies tightened their grasp on the Pacific arena, rations were cut and cut until we were surviving on half our original inadequate allowance. I lost weight and my energy levels started to fall. Malnutrition was evident in the faces around me. Clothing had been patched and mended until it was reduced to rags. And in the shadows of our minds prowled an unanswered question. Would our guards allow us to live if they came under attack?

On Wednesday, 15 August 1945 another notice appeared on the Bulletin Board: "The war is over... the Emperor of Japan has pronounced the cessation of fighting... a B29 bomber has dropped an atomic bomb on Hiroshima City." The detail was extraordinary. We had never heard of a B29 bomber, nor an atomic bomb. Excited and fearful, a crowd gathered in the courtyard in front of the Camp Commandant's office, demanding to know the truth.

"Is it over?"

"Is the war over?"

Finally he emerged and faced us. "I do not know. You should go back to bed."

Emboldened by the news, we laughed at him – but maybe he really didn't know. "Defeat" was not part of his vocabulary, and if he had never heard the Emperor speak before, who could say who had spoken these words?

On the Friday, around 9.30 a.m., as I walked back from breakfast to my dorm in the hospital, I heard the drone of a single aircraft approaching the camp. A B24 Liberator, clearly identified as American, flew into sight at around 2,000 feet. Internees grabbed Union Jacks and Stars and Stripes they had hidden away and gathered in their hundreds to attract the attention of the plane. Minutes later it passed overhead again, much lower at 500 feet, the noise of its engines hammering home the message to our captors – *the war is over*. Euphoria spilled out onto Main Street, onto Tin-Pan Alley, onto every lane, avenue and cul-de-sac. Anywhere and everywhere people were out in the open, all of us looking skyward, all revelling in that moment.

Then, to our astonishment, we witnessed seven bodies tumble at this low altitude out of the belly of the aircraft and float on parachutes down towards the fields outside the compound walls. Such bravery was humbling. Seven men – the improbably named "Duck Mission" – risking their lives for us, with 200 armed Japanese soldiers watching their descent.

An ecstatic tide of uncontrollable pandemonium swept over us. I found myself running with dozens of others, running for the gates of the compound. Grim faced, the guards lifted their guns but the huge onrush of prisoners was too sudden, too overwhelming. We ignored them. We thumbed our big Western noses at them. Their day was over. I careered headlong into a sorghum field, pushing my way between the eight-foot stalks, pausing momentarily to remove thorns from my bare feet, then rushing on, yelling at the top of my voice like so many others: "Where are you?"

A GI stepped out in front of me, his pistol drawn.

"The Japs? Where are they?"

"Not here. In the camp. All of them," I responded breathlessly.

A gang of us followed the soldier to where his commander, Major Staiger, was issuing orders. The men had set up a machine-gun on top of a Chinese grave and their wireless operator was trying to make contact with the B24. One of them, a young man in his mid-twenties, stepped briskly towards us.

"James Moore, Ensign, US Navy. Is Pa Bruce here?"

Jimmy Moore had been at Chefoo just a few years ahead of my sister. Later I heard he had volunteered specifically for the mission.

The crowd of internees around the soldiers swelled as more and more located their "saviours". There was no containing our excitement. It was clear the Japanese were in confusion. All thoughts of a strategic entrance were abandoned. Two or three of the GIs were lifted on shoulders and the crowd headed back to the gates, where a brass band played a "victory march" – a medley of Allied national anthems they had practised in anticipation (an activity they had shrewdly disguised by omitting the melodies in formal practice). After entering the compound Major Staiger received the sword of the Camp Commandant as a token of surrender and made him responsible for our care and security until a larger contingent of US soldiers arrived.

I remained outside the compound, listening to the boisterous strains of "Happy Days are Here Again".[15] It was two years since I had been beyond the confines of our prison. It was nearly four years since I had known any degree of freedom. I walked down to the creek running past the camp walls, edging its way seaward. Above the walls I could see the third-floor windows of the hospital at which I had stood day after day and wondered if this day would come. We had fantasized about release. Now it had happened. How quickly our perspectives had changed.

I walked back through the open gates. Our confused guards, uncertain now of their futures, still stood there. At the kitchen I asked what was on the menu. Soup, bread, maybe some fruit. People had been sent to buy provisions. The chefs promised me a meal I would not forget.

I was free in many different ways. With the end of internment, I was not a prisoner of war. I was seventeen, no longer a child at school. I realized I now had the freedom to choose my own course in life. And that realization allied itself with a desire to see my family again. My first steps would be in the direction of Yunnan Province and Taku. I was determined to go home.

自由
Jiyu
(Freedom)

I spent the next few days deriving great delight in being able to walk in and out of the gates at will, strolling along straight country lanes for miles. For years I had toured the camp, forced to turn at each depressingly familiar corner of the compound and complete another circle, with nothing new ever coming into view. Dressed in a newly acquired GI uniform and army boots, and with money supplied by the Swiss Red Cross in my pocket, I shopped at the Chinese market in Weifang for sugar to make boiled sweets and explored the town's unfamiliar lanes and avenues.

The second wave of US soldiers arrived to organize our camp, evangelically intent on brightening up our miserable lives. The strains of "Oh, What a Beautiful Morning"[16] belted out of the PA system at the break of day – an unwelcome diversion that jarred nerves and irritated tempers at our Entertainment Officer's expense. We were far from ready for his brand of civilization.

Occasionally B29s would thunder over the camp, dropping oil drums of provisions into the fields. We were warned to wait until the drums had landed before running out to retrieve them. Nobody wanted to survive the deprivations of a POW camp and die beneath a deadly delivery of Spam! Competition from the Chinese for the contents, however, was fierce, so we did not always heed the advice. I remember a drum thudding into the soil just twenty yards from where I stood. On running over, I was sickened to find that the crumpled heap of metal was covered in blood. Fortunately, the contents turned out to be tomato soup and ketchup!

At other times I buried myself in a reading room full of magazines and papers dating back to 1941. I had been denied four years of my life, an interruption I still feel I have never adequately reclaimed and which has fuelled my ongoing appetite for the history of World War II.

"You gotta have authorization to travel," the US wireless operator informed me. "Every last kriegie wants to go home. No one's getting out of here unless they get permission from elsewhere."

"Can you send a telegram to my father in Yunnan?" I pleaded. "I haven't seen him for seven years."

My apparently absurd attempt to hitch a flight home was actually more pragmatic than emotive. I had seen the planes flying into Weifang with supplies, and I knew they were flying back empty.

A Major picked up our conversation. "You haven't seen your dad for seven years?"

"No."

"Yunnan's a long way, son. We can get you to Xian. After that you'd be on your own."

"I don't mind. I just need to get back."

"We have to get this guy to Kunming," he instructed the wireless operator.

The man bent over his machine and composed a telegram for me. "It'll go to the British Consulate. They'll have to get in touch with your father. Metcalf, you say?"

"George Edgar Metcalf. With the China Inland Mission."

My father's response arrived the next day. I was summoned to the admin office and found an American officer waiting for me.

"Pack your bags," he said. "We've a plane headed for Xian. Truck leaves for the airfield in ten minutes."

I sprinted to the hospital and stuffed my few possessions into a dilapidated duffel bag. I grabbed three of my friends and together we ran to the waiting truck. At the airfield there was no time for farewells – the plane's propellers were already turning. I was hurried onto the aircraft. Within minutes I was gazing down through a dust-smeared circle of glass at the diminutive figures of my friends, frantically waving their goodbyes. I had escaped – their turn would come.

This was my first flight and I watched in fascination as the fields of Shandong floated away beneath us until we crossed into Henan Province and followed the elongated coils of the Yellow River to Xian. At dusk, over the pale lights of the airport, we circled down to earth. I was given a meal and a bed for the night in a US Army tent.

Despite my hasty departure and lack of time for proper goodbyes, I was fortunate to get away from Weifang when I did. Unbeknown to my father, the General Director of CIM, Bishop Frank Houghton, had issued instructions that repatriation of mission personnel must be done in an orderly fashion. Whatever his reasoning, it was an edict not well received by parents, who were anxious to see their children again. So many of them were unsure how, or if, their children had survived the war. They, unlike my family, had to wait weeks to be reunited.

On my second day in Xian I ran into a stone wall of a

duty officer. "There's no way to get you on any plane out of here," he told me.

I had sat as patiently as I could by the transit desk, hoping for a flight to Kunming. He was not moved by my story. Fortunately a grey-haired veteran officer in the freight department heard of my plight and came to lend weight to my case.

"You have money?" he asked.

I shook my head. Money wasn't a luxury I had missed much. He took out his wallet and emptied it into my hands. His example caused great hilarity in the office, and several others pushed notes and coins at me. I finished up with eighty-seven dollars, and I had no idea what it was worth.

"Now," said my benefactor. "Let's sort this out."

"Stone Wall" was having none of it. There were no orders. There were no papers. There was no way…

Congeniality gave way to command. "I am taking responsibility for this young man. Find him a flight, soldier."

Stone Wall clicked into action. "Yes, sir! What shall I put him down as, sir?"

"OSS. Route him via Chengdu."

"Yes, sir!"

"Always pays to pull rank," the veteran laughed as he informed me of the change of plans.

"OSS?" I asked.

"Officers' Special Service. I'll guarantee there'll be no questions asked!"

Remarkably, he was right. Within a few hours I was in Chengdu awaiting my flight for Kunming.

From Chengdu we flew south, skirting the Great Cold Mountains of South Sichuan Province, crossed the silver track of the Yangtze River and then traversed the hills of Yunnan, where Taku lay, far below, secreted away from my sight. Part of me longed to be there, but my parents were in Kunming, heading back to Australia. It was dark by the time a jeep carried me through the lowly lit streets of the city and deposited me in a cramped alleyway outside a modest, typically Chinese gateway. I recognized the raised characters carved on the gate: "Zhong Guo Nei Di Hui" – the China Inland Mission.[17]

I banged on the wooden slats. "*Kai men! Kai men!*"

There were footsteps. And then the gate was prised open. For a moment my father, now an elderly man with white hair, peered into the dark, surprised to find three "American soldiers" at the door. I had forgotten that I was eleven the last time I saw him – a round-faced boy with unbroken voice, hair draped untidily across my forehead beneath my cap, wearing half-length trousers, my socks pulled high to my knees. Now I was a young adult. My face had lengthened to manly proportions. My dark brown hair was swept back from my forehead. I had stubble on my chin and I matched him for height. But my face was skeletal and my body emaciated beneath my uniform. I weighed only six stone.

"Father... it's me. Stephen."

Eagerly I was drawn into the courtyard and embraced by my father and mother, my drivers forgotten. My dad had walked down from Taku only two days earlier, just in time to get my telegram at the Consulate and send a reply before learning from his colleagues of Houghton's directive. They had received no word I was coming. I was led into the home to be welcomed by all the missionaries, who had been praying for my return. Wild rumours had abounded about the whereabouts and circumstances of the Chefoo children.

It must have been emotionally testing for other parents to see me arrive while their children were still in Weifang.

Ironically, I was again separated from my parents almost immediately. They had plans in place to return to Australia for a break from their work and left Kunming within forty-eight hours. I followed them over the "hump" of the Himalayas to Calcutta in an RAF C47 a day later.

If my first experiences of flying had bordered on breathtaking, this flight teetered at the perimeter of the perilous. Over the Mekong River we plunged into a storm. Strapped into canvas bucket-seats along the ribs of the plane, we were pitched around with all the poise of a paper kite in the unforgiving grasp of a gale. The engines roared and bellowed as our pilot forced us up above the storm, only for us to plunge 3,000 feet back into its belligerence as we tumbled into an air pocket. Our pilot changed tack, electing to drop yet further, so that we hedge-hopped in alarming fashion over the paddy fields of India, watching the ground rush up to meet us and then skipping away from danger into the air again. It was with some gratitude that we landed at Dumdum Airport,[18] twenty kilometres from the city, and learned that our fuel had just held out. A number of other planes had ditched into the rice fields.

In Calcutta I was taken to the Viceroy's Palace.[19] A domed mansion built under the supervision of Richard Wellesley, Governor General of India, in 1803, it looked as though it had been transplanted from the estates of England and plonked in Asia. It had been turned into a centre for the repatriation of prisoners of war. It was here that I began to learn of the horrors that so many others had endured at the hands of the Japanese in camps in East Asia. I was asked to speak with a young Australian. He lay dying on his hospital bed, listless. His face was fixed in a vacant stare, looking beyond me from the gaping craters of his emotionless eyes. His shrunken expression still haunts me. I held the thin flesh of his wasted fingers and tried to encourage him.

"You'll make it, mate," I said. "The nurse says you will. Your folks want you back."

The nurse told me they had sent home three bodies in coffins that morning alone. There was a struggle going on to salvage those who could find the will to live. A balding Scotsman told me he was glad he could thank God for saving him from hell. Two thirds of his battalion had died or disappeared. I had little cause to talk of my own tribulations. It was clear from the rows of dying men at the hospital that it had been an horrific war for many and I had, in some ways, been one of the fortunate ones. I walked back from the hospital to the repatriation centre a very sober-minded young man.

From Calcutta I was put on a plane to Colombo and from there shared a flight down to Perth on a B24 with a POW who had been captured by the Japanese in Malaysia. He had been a civilian pilot, but was in poor health. He had suffered with amoebic dysentery, dengue fever and malaria. His captors had suddenly disappeared and it was weeks before he and the other prisoners were picked up. Generously, he provided me with money, as my eighty-seven dollars had been exhausted in Colombo. He had plenty of back pay to spend, he said. He reckoned he had another month in him – "Maybe…" he said.

From Perth I flew to Sydney, from Sydney to Melbourne and from there to Adelaide, my destination. I arrived weeks before my parents even secured a passage out of India. I was a prisoner of war and therefore a priority case. They were

classed as civilians and must make their own way as best they
could. It was supposedly spring in Australia, but there seemed
to be little of the fresh Yunnan greenness I had anticipated. As
we flew down towards the runway, the scene was as dry and
as dismal as a desert. An Air Force jeep was heading into the
city. I begged a lift and some while later I was dumped on the
corner of a main thoroughfare, outside 1 Kilkenny Road – a
greengrocer's.

"That's it, mate," the driver assured me.

Tentatively I pushed open the shop door.

"I'm looking for Ruth Metcalf," I said.

The large, ruddy-faced man behind the counter glanced
up from his customer, wondering what an American
serviceman was doing in Adelaide looking for Ruth.

"Side door," he said, nodding in that direction.

The side door was opened by an elderly lady.

"I'm Stephen Metcalf, Ruth's brother. I'm looking for
her."

"Ruth's on duty at the infectious diseases hospital. We
don't see her much these days. Hospital's a way out." The
woman introduced herself as Ruth Hartley. "We thought you
were coming. Hadn't had any word, though."

Many years before, Miss Hartley had applied to the
China Inland Mission and was turned down. Her mother paid
for my mother to go to China and the family became loyal
supporters of my parents. I would be staying with her brother,
Geoff, and his wife, Marge, until I got sorted. Miss Hartley
phoned my sister at the hospital.

Ruth bombarded me with questions: "How is Mum?
Dad?... Where are they?... How did you get here?... Why
didn't you tell me you were coming?" She promised to get to

the house as soon as she could, and hung up.

I replaced the receiver. Without warning an uncontrolled flood of emotion engulfed me. I was standing in the hall of the home of complete strangers, crying – sobbing so hard that I could not speak. Whatever feelings I had buried in the coal-stained black soil of Weifang Civilian Internment Centre, they would no longer be denied. The tears washed the layers of grime from my travel-weary face and, for the first time in a long while, exposed the extraordinary rawness of my ordeals.

曲路

Kyokuro
(Winding Path)

I arrived in Adelaide on 6 November 1945, Melbourne Cup Day, and for the first few weeks I was guided along the winding path to post-war Western civilization by my hostess, Marge. She was keen to get me down to the Red Cross.

"You've nothing but that uniform to wear," she told me quite firmly. "We've got to get you in civvies."

The lady at the downtown offices of the Red Cross was intrigued to be serving her "first American"! I was bemused by the endless forms she gave me, received instructions to go to the Rations Office and was handed 100 Australian pounds. The man at the Rations Office was named Possingham – "Poss" for short. He provided my ration cards and asked if I needed a job. I was passed on to a Mr Grant, who steered Marge and I in the direction of the Myer Emporium, one of Australia's leading department stores. Here I was fitted out with employment, a sports coat, grey trousers, leather shoes, a stylish felt hat with a sizeable brim, and bags of clothing equal to my new status. I was to report for work on Monday, 12 November at 9 a.m.

What contribution I made to the profits of the Myer retail empire that Christmas, I don't know, but I proved popular with the ladies. It is doubtful these women were particularly impressed with my physique, though I rapidly

68

regained weight to fill out my first two-piece suit. They were more taken with my accent. I failed to latch onto Australian lingo and maintained my "posh" pronunciation. Customers would stop in the store to hear me speak and girls working in other departments were always ringing up to "chat". For my services to sales and entertainment value I received five pounds per week.

Finding a church proved more difficult. On Sunday mornings I went to the Methodist Church where the Hartleys worshipped and tried the Presbyterian Church at night. I went to the Brethren Hall for a while, but when it came to communion I was asked to leave because I hadn't been baptized. Finally, I wandered into the Salvation Army Hall and found this more to my liking, until their persistent attempts to get me to the front to "repent" drove me away. It was the same story wherever I went – an inability on my part to settle into whatever form of worship was on offer and a general lack of interest by the church in me as a person. No one seemed concerned with a teenager whom they didn't know. "Poss" was the only one to offer friendship, meeting me at a sandwich bar for lunch and inviting me to visit his sheep and diary farm, fifty miles outside of the city; but he wasn't a Christian.

My parents were stranded in Calcutta until the New Year. They found it impossible to get a ship out of India. In the end my mother had to write to the Australian Ambassador to secure berths on a boat to Australia. As they stepped down onto the railway platform at Adelaide we were at last reunited as a family – something that had been impossible for seven years and, before that, had not truly occurred since Ruth left Taku for Chefoo, save for a fortnight each Christmas.

Ruth and I were no longer children; those years had been

lost to school and the war. Ruth was busy holding down a responsible job at the hospital. I was now the tallest in the family and finding my feet as an adult. My parents were in looks and attitudes like grandparents. In her mid fifties, my mother's black hair had turned white and my father, at sixty-five, was at retirement age. We were strangers to family life and this period was brief, lasting no more than a few weeks, but I treasured the time as I began to understand what life had meant for my parents through all their long years in China and learned to respect the sacrifices they had made for the Eastern Lisu.

We found a large bedsitter, sharing the kitchen with two other families. I had to sleep in a lean-to, a small space with lattice windows, at the back of the property, but soon retreated to a room in the house next door. We attended a local Baptist church. I found employment as an apprentice to an electrical engineer, but it was clear from the beginning that I was being exploited. My dad and I went down to Adelaide University to enrol me on a dentistry course, but the new course started the following January. I was short of money and suffering with persistent headaches. When my parents told me they were going to move to Melbourne, I decided to get out of Adelaide and go fruit-picking.

Berri is situated on the north bank of the Murray River, around 170 miles upstream from Adelaide and a train and rickety bus ride away. In 1946 the region was hard at work quenching South Australia's thirst for wines. I arrived one morning in February with a whole parade of pickers and was grabbed by a farmer to work his orchards and help with fruit drying. Wages were good – 50 per cent better than Myer's, plus overtime. Basic board – very basic – was thrown in.

Beyond the farm fence lay the Australian bush, an endless uncultivated expanse of mallee scrubland punctured by short, slender-limbed eucalyptus trees. In the early mornings, before I pulled apricots from their branches, I watched kangaroos and emus going down to the river to drink. It was hard physical labour, but I eased into the quiet of the open countryside. The headaches I had endured in the city disappeared. I began to take stock of my life.

By this time I had found myself a girlfriend and was falling in love. Joy was two years older than me. She was a typist, the daughter of the Methodist family I had stayed with in Adelaide. Her elder brother was paralysed. In desperation the family had gone to a Pentecostal church where, to their utter incredulity, he was partially healed through prayer. After this, he was able to walk a little and use a wheelchair.

I had not intended to fall for Joy. She was engaging and friendly, slim with short, light-brown hair, a neat couple of inches shorter than me. She loved to "yabber" with my family and they enjoyed her company. She had hung around a lot, wanting to talk with me, and wrote long letters when we were apart. I was looking for friendship and her obvious feelings for me began to be reciprocated.

When harvesting ended after five weeks in Berri, I decided to go to Murrumbeena, a suburb in south-east Melbourne, where my parents had found a new home. I really wanted to see Joy in Adelaide before I left, but she was busy. Reluctantly, I took up an invitation to spend my last few days in Adelaide at a mission rally at the Methodist Central Hall. Church attendance was an essential part of my weekly routine, but, like many in their late teens and twenties, I had drifted in my personal commitment.

The speaker was quite famous – the Revd Lionel Fletcher, once known as the "Empire Evangelist", who had started out as an apprentice on a sailing ship, had done a spell as a miner and a journalist, and then became a Congregational minister. He had pastored churches in Adelaide, Wales and New Zealand and had led revival campaigns across the Commonwealth. From the moment he began to speak I was captivated. He was unsensational, humorous and he was talking directly to me.

At the close of the meeting, as thirty or forty others moved to the front for prayer, I prayed quietly. The mercy of God flowed into my life with a freshness I had not known before. For some while I had been following a succession of meandering byways, lacking direction, but now, at least, my spiritual objective was clear – I must walk the path God had prepared for me, wherever that led.

My parents, alongside their speaking ministry, had found employment in Melbourne, caring for an elderly gentleman of ninety-four in his spacious home. The environment was far more pleasant than our situation in Adelaide – an area of extensive scrubland served by a busy railway station and a parade of shops. I moved in and found night-shift work at the Olympic Tyre factory. I took advantage of the evenings and weekends to be with my father and thrived on his tales of his work amongst the Eastern Lisu. He still had a yearning to return to China to complete his translation of the New Testament into their language.

Suddenly and surprisingly, in October 1946, CIM accepted his application and he and my mum set out again for Taku. I didn't question the decision. My dad was still fit. Unmistakably, my parents felt this was God's leading. Ruth was also planning to go overseas, preparing for missionary work in North Thailand. Six months after settling in Melbourne, I was once again homeless and in need of work. Only the employment agency at Berri bothered to answer my applications, so I returned to the fruit farms.

On another trip down to Adelaide to see Joy, my visit coincided with the National Convention of the Christian Endeavour Movement. The congregation was huge and the music emotive. When the minister began his talk I was open to God's message for me.

"How will you use those extra four hours?" asked the preacher. Australia was about to change from a forty-eight-hour working week to forty-four. "Who will give them to God? Who will devote those four hours to serving God and not fill them with their own concerns and pleasures?"

Stirred by his challenge, I rose to my feet in answer to his appeal. And God, bless him, took me at my word. He had a job for me to do, but it was not one I had anticipated.

On my return to the Berri fruit farms I started going regularly to the Methodist Church across the street from my lodgings. One week my minister was short of a preacher for one of the four churches under his care. Mr Hunt, the voluble owner of a store in Berri and elder of a tiny church in the town, proffered his pennyworth: "Ask your own man, Steve Metcalf. He's a budding preacher."

I was no such thing. I had only preached once before in my life and that was some weeks previously, when Hunt had bluntly told me I was speaking at his church. He hadn't waited for my protests. I had prayed a lot and preached a little to his congregation of eighteen people. I had no idea whether what I had said had been helpful.

On Hunt's flawed recommendation, my minister came

looking for me. "I need a preacher for Glossop Methodist," he explained.

"But…"

"I'm short on alternatives…"

I was short on excuses, and agreed to speak at the church the following Sunday.

At the close of the service the organist, an attractive young teacher by the name of Merl, a few years older than me, approached. She was pretty direct too. "You're the answer to my prayers," she said.

I was nonplussed. I couldn't for the life of me see where this was leading.

"I want you to start a Christian Endeavour group in Berri," she explained.

It was almost as though she and the store owner knew I had committed my spare time to God.

"I'm getting married, but I'll give you all the support I can," she promised.

Together we established a young people's group of thirty or more, many of whom became Christians. It was the beginning of a rich period in my life where I found real purpose.

角を曲がる

Kadowomagaru
(Turn a Corner)

It is fascinating, in hindsight, to see God's gentle guiding that brought me to a decision to go to Japan. At Eric Liddell's funeral I had decided that was what I must do, but, as I struggled to establish myself in Australia, the idea had faded. I had significant hang-ups over becoming a missionary. My exodus from China had left me bereft of all that was familiar. Integrating into the alien aspects of Australian society was a challenging process for which I had no preparation. I had found myself again turning at all-too-familiar corners and finding nothing new.

By now Joy and I were meeting frequently. We had been going out together for eighteen months. Our love for each other was deepening. Joy was ready to get engaged. I was more cautious. I was not yet twenty and strapped for cash. In June 1947, we attended a missionary rally run by twelve men, all around my age, from Melbourne Bible College. They preached, sang and gave their testimonies. The message stirred my thoughts about missionary service again. I told Joy how I felt. She was not enthusiastic.

"It would mean learning another language," she said. "I wouldn't like living in a foreign country."

It was on this difference that our relationship floundered. The following spring, Joy came to Berri for a week. We discussed at length engagement and my growing desire to serve as a missionary. Nothing was resolved. A few days after her return to Adelaide a letter arrived. The contents were devastatingly brief. Joy could not contemplate becoming a missionary wife. Her other friends were married. She had found someone else – a good friend, who had admired her for a long while.

I rang her. We talked. But whatever love she had harboured for me had drifted away because of my desire to go overseas. When I put the phone down I knew that Joy would not go with me and I was heartbroken. For a week I was physically sick, confined to hospital with enteritis. For three months I stumbled from work to ministry with the local youth and back again, hiding the desolation that had undermined my dreams for the future. I could not pray. Locked in my own feelings of loss, I shut out family and friends until Ruth demanded that I write to my parents.

I met Joy twice more before sailing to Japan. One evening, while down in Adelaide to attend a CIM conference on missionary work, I jumped on the convention bus and in the semi-darkness eased myself into the last empty seat. To my disbelief, Joy was sitting alongside me. A tangle of thoughts and emotions teased me. Perhaps... Slowly I moved to take her hand, but she pulled it away gently.

"Things have changed, Steve."

She lifted her hand slightly and in the fleeting illumination from the roadside I saw her engagement ring.

Joy prattled on while I tried to compose myself. It was clear that whatever affection she had felt for me was firmly consigned to the past.

"I've a friend I'd like you to meet," she said. "She's

thinking about full-time service. You'll like her."

Her friend proved to be stunning and a beautiful singer, but there was nothing in our conversation to attract me. I resolved to put this episode of my life behind me and took encouragement in a conversation with Oswald Sanders, CIM Australia's Home Director.

"I'm thinking about missionary service, Mr Sanders."

His recommendation was to go away and put a few years of maturity on my life. "Otherwise you'll be off to Bible College and it'll all be academic. Read some good Christian books."

He reeled off a list of worthy tomes while I wondered whether my budget would stretch that far.

"You need a clear call to the mission field. Being the son of Eddie Metcalf isn't enough."

He also had advice about women: "And stay clear of a marriage partner until you've sorted out your language study on the field."

In the circumstances I was not in a rush to give my heart to anyone. I did heed this, and his other advice, but in retrospect it was one piece of missionary wisdom I wouldn't necessarily pass on to new recruits.

Committed now to missionary service, I began to take every opportunity to learn more. A talk about Bolivia by the first principal of Adelaide Bible College, Revd Allan Burrow, whose parents worked in South America as missionaries, was another stirring experience. I began to pray that God would send me wherever he wanted. My desire was to return to the mountains of south-west China. This was home. The Eastern Lisu were the people with the greatest claim on my life. I knew Mandarin Chinese and had learned the Lisu language as a child. It was common sense to apply for service in China. But God was not going to release me from my pledge at the graveside of Eric Liddell.

Japan's defeat in 1945 had come through the strategies of the Supreme Commander for the Allied Powers of the Pacific, Douglas MacArthur. In victory the USA had handed him control of the occupying administration in Tokyo. MacArthur was well aware of the religious nature of Japanese society and the damage that defeat had inflicted on the spiritual status quo. "Japan is a spiritual vacuum," he had told a group of American clergy, invited to his headquarters in the Dai-ichi Insurance building in the capital, in October 1945. "If you do not fill it with Christianity, it will be filled with communism. Send me a thousand missionaries." In a radio broadcast two years later, on 24 February 1947, MacArthur told the American Congress (in error) that 2 million Japanese had been converted "as a means to fill the spiritual vacuum left in the Japanese life by the collapse of their faith."

One evening in my shack in Berri, I listened to MacArthur speaking on the radio about the need in Japan for the gospel. His words struck me with all the force of God himself speaking. I could not ignore the message. China, under Communist rule, was closing its doors to missionaries. Japan now began to feature more and more in my quest to serve as a missionary. In 1950 I enrolled at Melbourne Bible College and discovered that my room-mate was heading for Japan. His enthusiasm was both a challenge and an encouragement.

Another significant inspiration was an address given by Revd Leslie Gomm at the college. His son had gone missing in action in New Guinea. Gomm had joined the Australian Army in Japan as a chaplain in an attempt to find out what had happened to him. Sadly, he learned, his son had been killed but he was unable to locate the grave.[20] This was the first time I had heard someone speak compassionately about mission in Japan. So many Australians were distressed by the stories from the war and there was little love lost on the Japanese. Even some Christians were openly antagonistic.

As my Bible training came to an end I began to apply to a number of missions to serve in Japan. One turned me down and the other two pointed me back in the direction of CIM. The mission had been forced to withdraw from China with the victory of the Communist army over the Nationalist government. Now the leadership was carrying out surveys of other countries and recreating itself as the Overseas Missionary Fellowship (OMF). My father, despite his long service with the mission, was not keen for me to join.

"They've no experience of Japan. There'll be problems until they establish themselves. You should look elsewhere."

His advice was prophetic, but I knew I should be working for OMF. I applied for placement in Japan. Although my call was clear, the mission at that time would only accept open offers of service. Would I be prepared to go elsewhere? It seemed that mission policy had to be put before my convictions. God, thankfully, was one step ahead. The new workers in Japan requested young men to be sent as soon as possible. I was accepted. Arrangements were made for my departure out of Brisbane on the *SS Taiping*.

In leaving I said my final farewell to Joy. There should have been little significance in it; after all, it had been four years since I last spoke to her. But perhaps I had not allowed for the depth of my feelings for her. With both Ruth and I travelling to Asia, a meeting was organized in Adelaide. The hall was packed with well-wishers and prayer partners. As I rose to give my testimony, I froze. Joy was standing to one side of the hall. My emotions choked me. I stuttered my way through my presentation, totally disorientated by this turn of events. Afterwards Joy and her mother came over. They wanted my prayer letters and would be praying for Ruth and me. And then Joy was gone. This painful chapter of my life had been brought to a close.

污點

Oten
(Stain)

Monday, 17 November 1952 was a starless night on Australia's east coast. At midnight a few sharp shouts rose from the "wharfies" on the quay at Brisbane docks. The engines of the *SS Taiping*, my passage to Kure in Japan, shuddered and the old tub creaked and groaned as she eased herself, like a grumbling arthritic, away from her berth. We laboured downriver towards Moreton Bay and the hazards of the Great Barrier Reef. Ahead there was the heavy mantle of night waiting to envelop our ship. As the lights of the city began to thin and fade, I leant on the railing outside my cabin and prayed, "Make me a beacon of light. A light that streams out into the stormy darkness, in a place where lights are so few and far between."

The *Taiping* seemed like the original slow boat to anywhere. Just over 100 metres long, she had a cluttered, functional appearance: a high-chested central stack of second- and first-class accommodation slotted between two towering masts, one fore, above the cargo hold, the other aft. Apart from the regular fare of the dining-room, there were few facilities to amuse the small number of passengers.

Built in Hong Kong in 1925 for the Australian-Oriental line, she had done ample service plying the seas between Manila and Melbourne. She was among the last ships to sail out of Manila harbour in 1941, evacuating women and children to the sanctuary of Australia after Japan had bombed American airfields in the Philippines, and possibly the one Ruth and her friend, Betty, escaped on.

Six years later the *Taiping* was the first vessel from Sydney to Japan carrying Australian wives and children to be reunited with their husbands and fathers after the war. Between these two missions the boat was requisitioned by the Royal Australian Navy as a "Victualling Stores Issues Ship", part of its "China Fleet", supplying Allied warships as far away as the coasts of Africa and the Mediterranean.

Our first stop was the island of Tarakan, which lies on the east coast of Borneo in the Indonesian Archipelago. In the harbour the wreckage of Allied landing craft was still evident alongside broken jetties. The docks were awash with well-equipped Indonesian troops. They had little good to say about their wartime rulers, the Japanese, nor about their former colonial masters, the Dutch. The townsfolk were a noteworthy assortment of nations – indigenous Indonesians alongside Indians, Malays and the ubiquitous Chinese, who owned the shops and businesses. On the dusty streets I encountered an incongruous mix of the wealthy with tribal men and women who had apparently walked straight out of the jungle. There was an all-pervading pong of dried fish from the open market, where adults and children chewed on betel nut or, with red-stained teeth, stripped layers of sugary pith from sticks of dark-green sugar-cane.

To fill the time I took a bus ride out to the oil fields in a converted jeep with a canvas hood. The Tarakan oil wells had been fired twice during the war. First by the Dutch, as the Japanese assault forces attacked, and then, three years later, by Allied bombing. Though the oil fields were now back in production, heaps of old rusting machinery were slowly being sucked beneath the canopy of encroaching jungle.

For the most part our voyage from Tarakan to the Philippines was uneventful to the point of boredom. There were only eight second-class passengers, including myself, to fill forty-eight berths, and we had room to bulge in any direction. My cabin came complete with three beds and a small hand-basin, which afforded hot and cold water. The passengers met at mealtimes, sharing our conversation with the ship's dozen or so officers. But for the main part we idled northwards, occasionally spying land, thankful for a breeze to relieve the oppressive humidity, relishing the sunsets that lavished colour across the darkening skies.

Post-war Manila was a complete contrast to the deprivation of Tarakan; it was a piece of modern America displaced onto the rim of the South China Sea. Ranks of American-made cars and trucks clogged highways flanked by rows of impressive buildings. Among the older Spanish-styled houses I was amused to discover that my Filipino counterparts serenaded their prospective wives from the street while their beloveds sat by the barred windows of their homes. Given my recent experiences, I was in no hurry to adopt this alternative approach!

As at Tarakan, there was still plenty of evidence of the war. When the Allies drove the occupying forces out of the Philippines, many Japanese ships had been bombed, strafed with gunfire, sunk or blown out of the water in Manila Harbour. Its waterways were still blocked by the rotting remains of useless hulks. Here, however, the Japanese had returned, this time to salvage their vessels and transport them back to Japan.

We sailed through a storm to the welcome shelter of Hong Kong Island. In the first shadows of nightfall the mountainside was radiant with row upon row of tiny lights; a reminder of the lights of Brisbane I had left behind six days before. The British colony was burdened with refugees. With the victorious Communist government consolidating its power in China, hundreds of foreign missionaries had been making their way out to Hong Kong. But there were also tens of thousands of Chinese refugees, rich and poor, squeezed into shacks in the villages beyond the city centre or held in sprawling squatter camps. With an abundance of missionaries in Hong Kong, it had not been difficult to establish a ministry amongst these people. Hundreds of Chinese, having lost all they possessed, were fervently receiving Christ.

When I returned to the *Taiping* three days later, I found that the comfortable world of my own cabin had gone out of the porthole, so to speak. The lower decks were crammed beyond capacity with British soldiers. Somehow 300 conscripts on National Service were sharing a space meant for 100, while their officers found room with us in second class. These novice soldiers, dressed in their pristine uniforms, were 18–20 year-olds headed for war – recruits to the United Nations forces in Korea.

In June 1950 Communist North Korea had launched a shock artillery attack on South Korea, her troops flooding over the border (the "38th Parallel"), overrunning Seoul and much of the country. The UN, principally reliant on American forces, had pushed the North Korean army back in a strategy which also threatened China's borders. Now the opposing armies – the United Nations against an alliance of China and North Korea – were literally entrenched in a grim echo of World War

I warfare: token ground gained then lost, lost then regained.

Britain had never entertained much enthusiasm for the fight. Sapped by post-war austerity measures, people had lost interest in a campaign that could not be won on the battlefield and was continuing at the expense of British lives while obdurate politicians bartered month after month over the exchange of prisoners of war. To bolster its depleted army, the British government had extended National Service to two years. These new recruits were receiving the equivalent of £1.62 per week to face deprivation and death.[21]

Time has erased my memories of the faces of the young men I spoke with. Among them was a Quaker. "Are you the only missionary on this ship?" he asked.

"Yes."

He shook his head. "All these soldiers going to make war. And only one person to make peace."

Others were less understanding. Most were staggered to learn that I had been a prisoner of war and yet was determined to go to Japan.

"You're an idealist," they scoffed.

Perhaps, to them, I was. My experience of incarceration as a POW was not the catalogue of abuse suffered by some, but it had been no holiday camp. And I had another vivid recollection of Japanese barbarity that had left a mark on my memory; one of those marks not easily removed.

West of Hong Kong, along the Chinese coast, is the peninsular port of Beihai. In December 1938, its harbour was a bustling place, an intriguing fusion of activity.[22] I was eleven, one of a bunch of excited boys in school caps and short trousers, playing endless games of hide and seek, in a party of around fifteen kids returning from Chefoo for Christmas at home. The harbour was too shallow for our ship, the SS *Canton*, to dock, and we had anchored 300 yards from the quay while Chinese junks plied back and forth, unloading and reloading cargo – everything from squealing pigs trussed up in wicker baskets to crates of weird tropical fruit and colossal hessian sacks of rice.

The distant drone of aeroplanes brought the boys out onto deck, scuttling fore and aft, trying to spot the aircraft. There were six of them moving at speed. I counted them.

"It's the Japs!"

"Fighters!"

And then they were on us, whipping like wild winds across the harbour, opening fire on the fishing boats and junks.

In a few minutes what had been the ordinary hum of a small harbour at work was turned into a melee of churning water and flailing bodies. The guns in the sky above me spat and clattered, tracing lines of holes in sails and splintering wood. Bullets thudded into their targets or jounced away and smacked into the water. Chinese sailors and dock-hands swarmed to find shelter. For many it was hopeless to hide. Caught in the open, there were no safe places. I heard the harrowing cries of those who felt the impact of bullets and fell. There was no return of fire. The attackers emptied their magazines at will and flew away.

The deck of our small French steamship was crowded with passengers, dumbfounded by the swiftness of the attack, appalled at the callousness of the action. Our Chinese crew exploded into anger, loud voices demanding an answer. How could anyone shoot at innocent fishermen on boats that represented no military threat?

Shock rippled through me. All my boyish play-acting of war could never prepare me for the appalling reality that had been executed in Beihai Harbour. I was old enough to know that the Japanese soldiers who patrolled the streets outside my boarding-school were China's enemies. But this atrocity seemed nonsensical. The victims were just ordinary folk; people who waved to us from their boats and asked our age and where we lived. Mesmerized by the events, I gaped up into the empty sky after the planes and then down at the destruction. Almost subconsciously, I became aware of the shouts of captain and crew to weigh anchor. Our ship turned on its keel and headed out to sea, leaving the wreckage of the harbour behind as quickly as her engines would allow.

I cannot and will not forget the horror of those few moments. My empathy naturally lay with the Chinese. The Japanese were the aggressors. At the age of eleven, it was no more complicated than that. And so it remains. But any lasting antagonism towards the Japanese has been transformed into love.

From Hong Kong the *Taiping* sailed up the Taiwan Straits, across which Chinese Communists and Nationalists were still at war. During my voyage I had seen some heart-rending things. The damaged oil fields of Tarakan. The choked harbour at Manila. The pitiful squatters in Hong Kong. The bleak prospects for soldiers bound for Korea. They were all appalling reminders of the destruction of lives and of livings that war brings.

入口

Iriguchi
(Doorway)

A hundred thousand yen – that was the reward for slipping on a belt of Swiss watches and getting them through customs. The Chinese cabin crew pressed me hard to take them.

"Two. You take two."

"Two hundred thousand yen. Good money!"

"Good money. No problem."

The *Taiping* was, no doubt, not the only ship being used to smuggle contraband into Japan that autumn. In the years immediately after the war the black market had grown into a major industry, until the occupying administration had addressed the population's needs.

I refused to take the watches. I hadn't come to Japan to benefit myself, I told them.

My cabin-mates said I was stupid. They were going ashore to entertain themselves in the *ryokans* – local inns – with lissom, kimono-clad young women. Instead, on leaving the ship, I boarded a bus crammed with Japanese and headed out of Kure along the coast to Hiroshima.

On the morning of 6 August 1945 this port on the south-west shore of Honshu, the largest of Japan's islands, had wakened from slumber and stirred itself for work. The city served as a minor supply and communications centre for the war effort, imparted its industrial weight to the cause and ran a number of military camps for defence troops. With the capture of island after island, the Allied forces had beaten a determined path northwards along the length of the Pacific, coming within striking distance of the Japanese mainland. American bombers had pounded the life out of the majority of Japan's cities, but calls for unconditional surrender had been rejected. Hiroshima had remained largely unscathed. That Monday morning was still, with a clear blue sky.

Early warning radar picked up the approach of foreign planes around 7 a.m. There were anxious glances skyward. Tension tightened as the aircraft, slivers of silver cruising at 26,000 feet, inched into sight. Reconnaissance, most likely, was the prevailing view. The "all clear" sounded. At 8:15 two B29s appeared and, as people set out for work, one of these bombers, the *Enola Gay*, untethered "Little Boy", a uranium-235 isotope bomb given birth by the USA's Manhattan Project.

The device, a blunt-nosed torpedo the length of a small car, was not designed to fall to ground under its own weight. Furnished with a parachute, it floated silently downwards. It is doubtful that many of the citizens of Hiroshima would have even noticed it. It was a minute, unidentifiable lump of grey metal swinging serenely at the end of its reins. Certainly none of them could have imagined the utter annihilation it housed.

It took less than a minute for the bomb to fall from the sky. It exploded at around 600 metres above the ground. Unimpeded by buildings and topography, the discharge radiated destruction in every direction. From the epicentre a solid pillar of dark smoke with a central scarlet thread reared upwards, thrusting into the air an overarching ball of broiling dust and debris. Inexorably the scarlet core expanded outwards, consuming its black sheath until the whole terrible column glowed red. It was the most powerful explosive ever to be unleashed against man and his environment by other men. In mere seconds, Hiroshima suffered destruction on a scale that only relentless carpet bombing could have emulated.

Survivors of the blast spoke of being blinded by blazing lightning, of their world swept into oblivion by sirocco winds heated to hellish degrees, of being deafened by the rumblings of deep-throated destruction. Battered, bewildered, they were flung into a future that their past could never have prepared them for. They had no comprehension of what had happened and no conception of how they must deal with its consequences. In that moment Japan's faltering imperialism died and, in one of World War II's supreme ironies, the nation that the Western world declared to be the epitome of remorseless barbarism was transformed, in its own eyes, into the world's most mortified victim.

There were no hiding-places in Hiroshima. The city had developed on the flat shores of a river delta where the Ota River glided unhurriedly into the waters of Japan's Seto-Naikai, the Inland Sea. Divided at the mouth of a valley of small hills into a fan of seven channels, the river passed placidly beneath countless broad bridges and bore passenger ferries and fishing boats with white sails on its back. On the river-banks densely packed neighbourhoods of wooden houses pressed up against low-rise brick and reinforced-concrete shops, schools, offices and hospitals.

In a report in the *London Express* on 5 September 1945, William Burchett, an Australian journalist who visited Hiroshima four weeks after the event, described the bomb damage as making "a blitzed Pacific Island seem like an Eden". The Imperial Palace had been reduced to "a heap of rubble three feet high, and... one piece of wall". He described "chimneys without factories" and "three miles of reddish rubble", and surmised that "a monster steamroller... [had] squashed it out of existence". Photographs show a plain of debris stretching as far as the sea, etched with the pinched lines of the city's major streets, interrupted only by the shattered skeletons of a few surviving structures.

Those closest to the explosion vanished. The destruction left no tokens for identification, no traces of existence, no ashes to collect. As the survivors, the *Hibakusha*, surfaced from the wreckage of their homes and offices, many discovered that they were naked; their clothes had been scorched from their bodies. Some carried imprints of fashion designs tattooed onto their burnt skin. Bleeding from wounds they scarcely knew they had received, their flesh ripped aside to expose muscle tissue, their limbs cracked and crushed, they stumbled and crawled over the rough wasteland of ruin in the direction of the demolished hospitals. Their bodies burned. Insufferable thirst consumed them. A sulphurous odour assaulted their nostrils. The air was choked with yellow dust. The sun, a symbol of their nation, was lost behind swirling ash-laden murk. Fires wrapped themselves around the relics of wooden structures. Long-limbed pine trees burned, bowed their heads and fell. Flames spewed from the earth – the spontaneous combustion of concealed "kindling". The *Hibakusha* moved in silence, struck dumb by the trauma they had endured.

On 9 August another B29 bomber dropped the rotund "Fat Man", a plutonium-239 device nearly twice as powerful as the Hiroshima bomb, onto the industrial areas of Nagasaki, and Japan kowtowed to the concept it had banished from its collective consciousness – defeat.

My bus from Kure Harbour pulled into Hiroshima and I alighted at the station. I was astonished to find there was little evidence of the devastation that I have described. Newspaper reports painted a bleak picture, but the sights that greeted me were very different to what I expected. In the seven years since the war the city had been resurrected and had absorbed its nightmares.

It seemed as though half the population was on the move. Small Datsun taxis and three-wheeled trucks weaved in and out of the bustle of traffic. Men pulled handcarts laden with goods or pushed bicycles precariously loaded with merchandise along crowded streets. Pedestrians carried packages and parcels in *furoshiki* – pieces of cloth, large and small, cleverly arranged to hold a purchase, whatever its shape and size.

I was shocked to find packed beer halls and people gambling away their earnings at slot machines. I was appalled at invitations to enter brothels. Housing had been erected in long barrack-like blocks, shabby dwellings laid out in monotonous ranks. Ten families lived in one of these rows of single rooms, with a compact kitchen and toilets constructed at one end. It was the same all over Japan, I was told.

At the divide of the Ota into the Honkawa and Motoyasu Rivers, the T-shaped Aioi Bridge spans these three watercourses. The surrounding area had been Hiroshima's administrative, commercial and political heart. The bridge had been the intended target of the bomb. At that time there were few memorials associated with the bombing to see. I was guided in the direction of the "A-bomb Dome", an exhibition hall designed by a Czech architect, Jan Letzel, thirty years before. Some of the walls had survived due to its location beneath the blast, as had the metal framework of its dome – a feature that has come to symbolize the destruction. Around it the locals had set up exhibits of the disaster. The most disturbing of these was a concrete step bearing the image of a man burnt into the surface. The actual epicentre of the explosion was a block away; another cruel irony of war. Scientists had used the direction of shadows caused by heat rays to calculate that at the very centre of the circle of destruction lay 29-2 Saiku-machi, the Shima Hospital.

A Peace Memorial Park was being created on the triangle of land at the fork in the Ota River. Along the river-bank I found a neatly sculptured earthen memorial mound. Bodies pulled from the river and ruins were brought here for cremation. Beneath this, a vault now houses the ashes of 70,000 victims, some of which are still unclaimed today. Opposite this were the remains of a sizeable three-storey kimono shop. The roof had been pushed inwards and the interior gutted. Remarkably, some staff had escaped, though all but one man, who was in the basement, consequently died of their injuries. Beyond this stood another monument, an arch-shaped cenotaph representing the sanctuary of an ancient Japanese home. Within its walls there is a stone chest containing a register of the names of people who were killed at the bombing of Hiroshima and those who died subsequently as a result of the radiation. With no partiality for nationality or status, these books currently contain over 200,000 names. At the south side of the park, by the Peace Bridge which would take me back over the Motoyasu River, stood a monument surrounded by a low wall – a tribute to over 600 pupils at the Municipal Girls' School, the largest death toll suffered by any of the city's schools. Carved on the front panel is a picture of

93

three girls. The central figure carries a box bearing the formula "E=MC^2" – an indirect reference to "atomic warfare" (a term prohibited by the occupying post-war administration).

I walked back to the station and found the bus to Kure. I felt oddly impervious to the emotions I may have expected. All I could think of was how everything around me was extraordinary. It was all so unexpectedly different from China. It was only on subsequent visits that I was able to reflect on how the events here in August 1945 had secured my freedom from prison camp. There could be no joy in the obliteration of life, but my release and Hiroshima were undeniably linked.

By evening I was aboard the *Taiping*, sailing for Kobe. Here I would finally disembark and head for the mountain town of Karuizawa, "Light Spring Valley", west of Tokyo, where the OMF language school was located. I needed to begin a battle of my own. Somehow I had to learn Japanese. Otherwise the polite strangers who had greeted me along the streets of Hiroshima would remain no more than strangers.

よろめき

Yoromeki
(Faltering Steps)

Hataraku, hataraita, haraki, hataraite, hatarako, hatarakeba, hataraitara, hataraitari, hatarakaseru, hatarakareru, hatarakaserareru, hatarakeru, hatarakanai, hatarakanakatta, hatarakanakattara, hatarakanakattari, hatarakanakereba, hatarakanakute, hatarakazu, hatarakitai, hatarakitakatta, hatarakitaku, hatarakitakute, hatarakitakereba, hatarakitakattara, hatarakitakattari.

Hataraku – "to work". Twenty-six versions of a verb. Certainly more than enough to make a rookie to language learning sit up and take notice. The Japanese, I rapidly discovered, have an enormous capacity for words, without conveying a great deal. Books, which in English would fit into 100 pages, can consume three times the acreage of paper. Conversations lasting an hour can be translated into a matter of minutes. Where, for a foreigner, clarity would be beneficial, vagueness can pervade communication, ideas and beliefs. For a nation with an enviable reputation for efficiency – richly deserved – there can be a frustrating lack of finality. While the trains may run rigidly to time and industry may have the regularity of a metronome, this is matched by immense uncertainty in life.

I also discovered that the Japanese had become very eclectic – great borrowers from every nation. They had adopted the engineering and inventions of America, borrowed the best of British literature, embraced magnificent music from Europe and pocketed the fashions of France. Buddhism had been brought over from China and assimilated into their national religion, Shinto. They had no qualms about adding Christ into this pot-pourri of creeds. Inclusivity seemed the ideal. All these "bests" could be integrated into the "Big Best" – Japan.[23]

Around the time the Romans were vacating England, the Japanese were adopting complex Chinese characters, *kanji*, as their script. Pronunciation was aided by the introduction of syllabic "squiggles", *katakana* and *hiragana*. Clever arrangements of these systems, allowing a pantheon of word-plays, have become a great entertainment amongst the Japanese. Assimilation of foreign words, however, has not been limited to Chinese. One day, early in my language study, I walked the couple of miles into Karuizawa from the OMF mission centre and found a stationery shop. There was a pleasing tidiness about the place, an attention to detail, though apart from two sets of glass shelves behind the counter and a calendar hanging on the wall, there was little else to recommend it. The assistant, dressed in a plain, dark kimono, bowed slightly as I entered. I found what I was looking for beneath a glass counter. It was something of a relief not to mumble my way through an inadequate explanation of what I wanted. The woman was courteous and waited patiently while I assembled my paltry Japanese.

"*I–ku–ra de–su–ka?*" I pointed at a pen, "How much?"

"*Pen desu ka?*"

I was surprised at the assistant's knowledge of English. I nodded and picked out an eraser.

"*I–ku–ra de–su–ka?*"

"*Gomu desu ka?*"

"You speak French!" She shook her head and passed a notebook across for my inspection.

"*Notobukku desu ka?*"

The "yen" dropped. The lady had not studied European languages. It was simply an incorporation of Western words. Feeling pleased with myself, I paid and turned to leave.

"*Mata dozo.*" The assistant bowed with the same slight bend at the waist that had punctuated our brief conversation.

"*Ma–ta do–zo.*" I returned her bow. To my chagrin, she laughed. I hurried away, unsure of what had caused her such hilarity. Surely "*Mata dozo*" must mean "goodbye"? My dictionary said otherwise. The phrase literally meant "again please" – an invitation to return.

The town of Karuizawa was a three-and-a-half-hour steam-train ride north-west from Tokyo on very old and very hard seats. The town was lodged on a plateau, thickly wooded with silver birch, spruce, maples, oaks, walnut trees and willows, high within the central peaks of Honshu Island.

The early part of the journey took in dozens of small stations as the train wound its way along a vast river plain towards saw-tooth mountains. The late-autumn countryside hemmed in hamlets of flimsy wooden homes, each with a well-ordered garden cherishing the very last of the chrysanthemums. Roughly shaven farmers, their heads swathed in cloths and wearing plant-pot fur hats, worked the paddy fields alongside their wives, who were more neatly attired in fitted padded jackets and patterned pantaloons.

In the distance I could see Mount Asama, an active volcano, pushing grey feathers of ash into the air, her plumage rising high into the atmosphere and drifting to ground as a dreary coating of dust on the fresh snow. It was a view that "is wonderful to the extent that you can't say anything at all", as the Japanese would lengthily exclaim.

A second engine was hitched to the rear carriage, and we commenced a push-me-pull-you ascent of the slopes. The Japanese called it *suwichi-baki* ("switchy-backy") – another apt adaptation of "American"! We chugged up one grade, ready to reverse up the next; a zigzagging climb to the top via fifty-six hairpins. Finally, we entered a tunnel, emerged minutes later onto a mountain plateau and wheezed to a halt at our lofty destination.

The main town, numbering no more than 10,000 residents, was in reality a summer retreat for rich foreigners and a holiday location for the Japanese. Spacious European-style *hoteru* and houses had been hidden away amongst the trees. A number of missionary societies had congregated in Karuizawa for language study and the area enjoyed the services of three churches. Housing across the country was still scarce and the Japanese were not always eager to lease accommodation to the nations who had destroyed their homes in the war. OMF had rented the annexe of a dilapidated hotel and two eight-roomed homes, one of which acted as a school for missionary children, at the far end of the valley.

Whatever the attractions in the summer, in winter the place was quiet and cold. The overladen branches of the fir trees by our front door bowed low beneath a cumbersome burden of snow. A stream burbled through the hotel grounds, nibbling at the snow-drifts on its banks and shifting small trinkets of ice downstream. For weeks on end, beyond our frosted panes of glass we could only see an expanse of frigid white, undisturbed, unyielding. Our houses had been built for summer vacations and not for the severity of a

Japanese winter at 3,000 feet, I can assure you.

I was billeted in a three-room shack with two other new boys, Dave Hayman, an Aussie, and Doug Abrahams, a Brit. Dave and Doug were only too eager to show me around and impress me with their Japanese vocabulary, even if it had only been learnt that day.

My textbooks were a romanized primer issued by Yale University and a small book of essential Christian phrases, with a page of handy sentences to get me through the basics of everyday living. We were blessed with the very modern aids of a tape recorder and gramophone records.

I needed to learn religious language in four hours of daily private study, complemented by two hours of formal tuition with our Christian Japanese teachers. I was required to grapple with twenty new words per day, pronounce them correctly, understand their grammatical uses and utilize them in sentences. Our efforts would be monitored periodically in a series of exams that we must pass to progress. And I acquired my Japanese name – Sutepano Metekafu – or Sutepano-san, as I was respectfully known.[24] The latter was my mistake. Introducing myself as Stephen Metcalf, I had forgotten that the Japanese place their surnames before their Christian names.

"Miss Singleton, the housekeeper, made Dave go down town to do the shopping." Dave had strung some words he knew into this sentence. Our teacher was not impressed.

"You cannot say that. It is impossible. In Japan no woman can make any man do anything. She must request him to do something."

Thus we started to learn the fundamentals of Japanese culture, reflected in the language and encountered in our occasional forays into town. Male dominance was a feature of life, men assuming unquestioned lordship over women.[25] While we judged such patriarchal relationships inappropriate, it raised questions that dominated our conversations. We were three guys studying alongside eight single women and four couples. How could our female missionaries impact Japanese society? And more pertinently, why were men apparently reluctant to come out on the mission field?

After a few weeks I had to face the inevitable. I needed a haircut. I remembered that in Chefoo the barbers had often been Japanese. Their premises invariably had blue, red and white revolving lights. I soon spotted one on Karuizawa's main street, a parade of no more than twenty drab stores. I slid open the door and received a flamboyant welcome into the rather shabby surroundings. The owner rubbed his hands on his white coat, left his half-shaved customer, found me a seat and poured out a cup of green tea which was placed on the small table beside me. There were three men sitting at another table playing *shogi* – chess, Japanese style. Curling strands of cigarette smoke embalmed the players as they studiously shifted the pieces up and down the board. I watched as the barber shaved the head of his customer, before guiding him to another seat and offering him tea.

It was my turn.

I nodded and smiled at the barber's incomprehensible question, with no clue as to what he was saying. I had a horrible feeling he was asking if I too wanted to be shaved to my scalp. Nervously I sat down and watched his progress in the large mirrors. Thirty minutes passed. Forty-five. He was clearly in no hurry. Nearly an hour. I sensed with relief that he was close to completing the task.

Suddenly he swung the well-worn leather chair down

into a horizontal position and slapped a hot towel on my face. He followed this with a second one and then lathered my face with brisk strokes of a brush. A cut-throat razor hovered over me. I remembered I had shaved that morning, but then remembered that I didn't know how to tell him to stop. He diligently scraped away every last trace of hair – three times over. I felt as though he had removed every individual strand – root, follicle and all. When I was swung back into an upright position, my cheeks and neck glowed pink. I was startled to find a woman sitting in the seat next to mine, also being shaved!

Still the process was not finished. The barber frenetically began hammering his fists into my shoulders and digging his fingers into my sore neck in a massage. Finally he inspected my haircut, snipped away any hairs that offended him, rubbed scented cream into my face, brushed me down, showed me to the table and poured me another cup of tea.

"*Mata dozo,*" he said earnestly as I made to leave. But I was learning, so I politely bowed and went back home to tell Doug and Dave my story. Ninety minutes in the barbers? For only seventy yen? (About seven pence!) Any self-respecting barber, I was informed, would have considered his customer slighted if he had offered less. Who was I to complain?

There was so much to learn. Bowing, it turned out, was an art form. Practice was needed to recognize the angle and depth of bow. Knowing who to bow to, when and how, was vital. Thursdays were reserved for eating meals in Japanese style. We knelt on mats around a low table and sampled a range of intriguing dishes with pointed chopsticks. Raised in China, I was, of course, a dab hand with these utensils. However, I was informed that, unlike the practice in China, the rice bowl should not be lifted to your mouth. The eating process suddenly became that much trickier. Kneeling with one's legs tucked well beneath one's behind was preferred, though sitting for a while with your legs to one side when pins and needles threatened was permitted. And then there was the sensitive subject of slippers.

The Japanese, like the Chinese and other Asian cultures, wisely remove their shoes when entering someone's home. The Japanese have developed the custom to a degree of slipper etiquette that is bound to fool the foreigner, no matter how hard he or she learns the rules. There are specific flat-heeled, open-backed slippers designated for all eventualities. Slippers for the hall or kitchen are not to be used in the living-room. Slippers for the living-room cannot be used in the hall or kitchen. One is supposed to slip with consummate ease from one pair to the next. And woe betide the unfortunate foreigner who wanders around a home with the bathroom slippers on.

Away one night from Karuizawa, I committed the ultimate *faux pas*. Exhausted from a day's travel, I settled down for an early night. Suddenly the silence was shattered by the blast of a trumpet and much beating of drums. Out of the window I spotted a "crier" accompanied by a band, all wearing advertising sandwich-boards. A group of merchants were setting up shop in the front room of the inn opposite, their wares spilling out onto the street. Here was a great opportunity for the gospel! I could give tracts to the whole village and save myself the trudge from door to door the next day. Eagerly I shrugged on a padded kimono and grabbed a pile of leaflets. Interest was high. People were falling over themselves to see what I was offering them. Rookie or not, this was missionary endeavour made easy! I would definitely have a story to tell Doug and Dave. As the salesmen finally began to clear up, I approached one of them and offered him a leaflet.

"In your country you wear shoes indoors," he commented.

"Yes."

"Even in your living-rooms?" He had chosen his words with immense care, but I was aware he was looking at my feet. I followed his gaze. Embarrassment consumed me. I had slippers on in the street! And, transgression of all trespasses, this pair had "WC" marked on them! I hastily retreated to the sanctuary of my room to assign slippers to their very proper places. Some lessons were learned the hard way.

On another occasion I was again out in the country and stopped at a small town for the night. I found a little inn fronted by a shop that seemed to sell almost everything. I enquired about accommodation and was shown to a pleasant upstairs room. I asked about an evening meal.

"I'm afraid there's nothing."

I was puzzled. My previous experiences had led me to believe that supper and breakfast were always provided. I asked again.

"Nothing. I'm sorry."

In stumbling Japanese I said I would go out to eat. A nearby restaurant provided a bowl of *udon* – thick noodles, steaming hot – and I returned to the inn to be informed that my bath was ready. Afterwards I found a low table in my room set with several dishes of food. Perplexed, I waited until my hostess appeared with a lacquerware bowl of rice and a bronze kettle of hot water.

"I'm afraid there's nothing," she told me again. "Please eat plenty."

My bafflement was complete. It was only later I found out that my hostess was politely playing down the quality of her cooking. I was supposed to counter her politeness with an overstated compliment. Nevertheless, my puzzlement at this particular inn was far from over!

My sleep was disturbed by an odd sound that I could only liken to bubbles bursting around my head. Unable to settle, I eventually got up from my floor mattress and turned on the light. On a shelf behind me was a row of wooden tubs with closed lids. The eerie effervescence was definitely coming from these small barrels. Cautiously I lifted one of the lids and was ambushed by a sharp aroma – the acrid smell of fermenting pickled Chinese cabbage and turnips.

I turned my bed around and settled once more, only to be disturbed by an old grandmother outside my room. She was clearly distressed about something. Me! My hostess appeared and chaotic commotion ensued until my mattress was returned to its original position. "Your head points in the wrong direction!" the lady instructed me firmly.

My teacher found the episode hilarious.

"How can one's head point in the wrong direction?" I asked.

"Only corpses are laid out with their heads towards the north," she explained. "The poor woman must have been quite traumatized."

I was up to lesson ten in my Yale primer when I failed my first exam. Our OMF language supervisor was not impressed.

"You will have to go back to lesson five and master the

basics," she told me. "You can't progress until you pass this exam."

Once again I had to face up to the fact that I was not a natural when it came to exams. I did not have my father's gift for languages. However, I had inherited my mother's talent for mimicry. A skill for which I had found little use at school now became a real asset. I could listen to words and with little effort repeat them. I began to fill my notebooks with the new words I heard, writing them down phonetically, then cross-checking in a dictionary to get them right. Slowly, over the next six weeks I slogged my way back to lesson ten and passed the exam. Though I never was a model pupil, that, thankfully, was the last exam I failed.

Two years of language study gave us the rudiments of Japanese. It was, however, like climbing in the local hills; every plateau revealed a new peak to conquer. When the time came to vacate our mountain retreat, I was still unable to read a Bible passage with real fluency. I couldn't write a letter and a simple reader for an eight-year-old could defeat me. I committed my Bible talks to paper in romanized script and was lost if I lifted my eyes from my prepared text. I sang hymns without knowing what I was singing. I had scarcely learned to understand what was said to me, let alone comprehend the subtleties of what was meant by what was said. But I was not in Japan for the short haul. In time I began to stride to the summits that soared way above my first forays into the foothills. And along the way God taught me that he could use the bluntest of instruments to construct the roads to his kingdom.

成果
Seika
(Fruit)

On Christmas Eve, 1952, Dave, Doug and I reserved one of the mission's cars, eager to get out into the local villages with gospel tracts. The car, as obdurate as a mule, refused to move. We tried for a while to cajole the engine into action. It was to no avail. Male pride had to be sacrificed. We ran back into the house and recruited a party of females to push us along the road until the engine stammered into life. The narrow roads were horrendous, an unremitting series of ruts, packed solid with frozen snow. But in the early morning we caught the first of the sunlight between the mountains and watched the sky lighten and settle to an unbroken blue. I was delighted to find tall, golden persimmon trees, denuded of leaves, their ripe, wrinkled, orange fruit clinging to the frosted, dark, hardwood branches – an image I treasured from my childhood in China.

We slithered our way from village to village, stopping to give out copies of the gospels.

"How much do they cost?" we were asked.

"Nothing," I replied. "Please. Take one."

In Japan, a gift places a future obligation to the giver on the recipient, and some people preferred to pay rather than take the small booklets we offered them. Most, however, were simply eager to see what the *Gaijin* (foreigners) were handing out, and we quickly exhausted our stocks.

Driven indoors by the cold, we found an eating house. We were soon warm again. We sat on cushions on the floor with our legs in a pit beneath the table where a small charcoal fire thawed out our feet. Our table was covered with a thick quilt which nestled around our knees. I ordered *tonkatsu* – thin strips of pork dipped in egg and breadcrumbs, deep fried, and served on top of a bowl of rice with onions and cabbage; one of my favourite dishes. The waitress provided *ban cha*, a dark-brown tea, and brought us sticky rice cakes. Afterwards, we retraced our route back to Karuizawa. It proved a hard day, but it whetted my appetite to get out and meet people.

Relieved of our studies in the holiday season, we went skiing in one of the local resorts. The town of Myoko was buried in snow, the houses' roofs barely showing themselves. I walked along "roads" level with the tops of street-lamps. Life, however, had not been lost beneath the snow. Adjacent to each property steps had been cut into the ice to allow the occupants up onto the surface. The shops were open. Cafés plied their regular trade. Children on small skis slalomed with their parents down the slopes. I lacked their finesse and spent much of my time tumbling rather than turning.

As night fell, Dave's future wife, Dr Rosalyn Ormiston, toppled over and we watched one of her skis slide silently away down the hill. Doing the expected thing, I gave chase. I was floundering around in the dark when two Japanese skiers appeared.

"Have you seen a ski?" I asked in Japanese.

"We'd understand better if you spoke English," the men responded tactfully.

So I spoke English. Before long I had forgotten Rosalyn's plight and was standing on Mount Myoko after nightfall, holding a lost ski, preaching to an audience of two – the strangest piece of evangelism I have ever done. Rosalyn, stuck up to her waist in snow, was greatly relieved when I eventually emerged triumphant from the dark.

At another resort, Akakura, I sat one evening by a fire, surrounded by a group of thirty or so, drinking tea and eating peanuts, giving my testimony in my pidgin Japanese with the aid of a pocket dictionary. My audience roared with laughter at my mispronunciation and mistakes, while I soldiered heroically on with my teaching. It was difficult to see that I was making any useful impression on them, let alone one of eternal significance. A few weeks later, however, I received a letter.

"You helped me…" the man wrote. "Your story impressed me and stirred my heart. I was an officer in the Japanese Army. As long as I live I shall never forget what you told us about the Bible on that snow-whitened mountainside. I am not a Christian, but after returning to Tokyo I am now reading my Bible. *Sayonara* – goodbye."

On another occasion our student group received an invitation to a sulphur mine from the manager's son. He had received a tract from one of our teachers and wanted us to speak to the miners.

"No religious people bother to visit us," he explained. "Not even the Buddhist priests."

He was keen that we should be well prepared. "They drink a lot. Sake. They are unrefined. Rough men."

And he was worried that we would make the journey safely. "It takes three and a half hours to get there. I will come to meet you and take you to the mine."

The pit train, an electric locomotive, ferried us into the

very heart of the hills. In the winter the area was cut off by six-foot snow-drifts and contact with the outside world was limited to a five-mile-long overhead-cable bucket conveyor, running from the mine to the railway terminus. The snow had melted and the area was alive with fast-flowing streams. I was reminded that in Japan it was impossible to be without a sight or sound of water. The hillsides were breathtaking, overlain with immense swathes of daisies, flaming red azaleas and wreaths of wild iris. The larger trees were covered in thick tresses of wisteria. Our walk from the railway station took us straight up the mountain slopes. I could not remember climbing so fast nor so far since I had left Yunnan.

At the end of our trek we were surprised to find a highly self-contained village of houses built on hillside terraces, with a school and a sizeable playing field. This was home to 300 miners and their families, living at around 6,000 feet above sea level. Thirty people turned up for the meeting. Dave used flannelgraph – Bible characters cut from felt, laid onto a simple cloth background – to tell the story of the Prodigal Son. Doug gave his testimony. It was the first time these people had heard the gospel. By the time we left, every scrap of literature was taken. In return we received a bouquet of rhododendrons.

As we commenced our walk back to the station, I was aware of the vast mountain plateau stretching out in all directions – a magnificent panorama hiding hundreds of similar villages in its deep valleys, places where the gospel had never penetrated. We seemed so few and they were so many.

One Saturday I filled a bag with tracts and gospel portions and caught the "switchy-backy" train down the mountain from Karuizawa, alighting at the city of Takasaki, twenty-five miles away. On a hill west of the city stands the statue of a stately woman, forty-two metres high.

"Who is she?" I asked.

"Kannon Sama," I was told. "The Goddess of Mercy."

Inside the statue's concrete shell there is a staircase winding upwards past numerous alcoves, which serve as booths for idols. At the top of the staircase there are windows that allow tourists views of the city. At the feet of the goddess were dozens of "Demetrius" (Acts 19:24) tradesmen sitting behind ranks of miniature silver statuettes. There was a zoo, a park and several temples for worshippers. I found a café serving meals of rice, pork and seaweed. When I gave the owner a tract, he and his wife presented me with a picture of the goddess as a gift to match mine!

"Where is the bus station?" I asked.

I was not always sure of the replies to my questions, but on this occasion I found the place without problem. Painted along the length of one wall was a mural depicting each of the villages and the bus stops along the route. From Takasaki I could take a bus to the terminus, where there was a mountain path back to Karuizawa. I decided this would be my way home again, rather than enduring the switchy-backy. I settled myself on a bench, waiting for the bus. A farmer's wife and her son were sitting opposite me, the boy holding a bamboo cage. They looked rather nervously at me.

"*Nan–de–su–ka?*" ("What is it?"), I asked, pointing at the cage.

The boy shied away and pressed against his mother.

"*Kirigirisu,*" replied the farmer's wife.

"*Ki–ri–gi–ri–su,*" I mimicked.

"*Kirigirisu.*"

"Ki–ri–gi–ri–su." I added the word carefully to the vocabulary list in my notebook. It meant "cricket". A nice rhyme with *Igirisu*, England.

"I'm a *Ki–ri–gi–ri–su jin* a cricket person," I joked, and the boy laughed.

"Kirigirisu jin!"

"What does your cricket do?"

"Naku." ("It cries.")

"Cries?" In Japan crickets cry.[26]

The village at the end of the bus ride was full of children eager to see the American who had just arrived.

"America! America!" they yelled at the top of their voices.

"No. English. *I–gi–ri–su jin!*" I shouted back, irritated by their error. Hoping to distract them from their chant, I repeated my joke. "I'm *Ki–ri–gi–ri–su. Ki–ri–gi–ri–su jin.*"

My play on words was lost in the laughter. *"Kirigirisu!"*

I tried to hand out tracts, but I rapidly became a Pied Piper, mobbed by scores of children shouting, "Cricket! Cricket!" Increasingly frustrated, I abandoned my attempt at missionary activity and headed to an inn for the night. The children were not to be deterred. They crowded around the windows and continued their chant. In the end the innkeeper called a local policeman, a middle-aged man, to drive them away.

"Where do you come from?" he asked.

I showed the policeman my registration card.

"Why have you come here?"

I handed him a copy of St John's Gospel. I had no idea if he had ever seen a Bible before. The man took it, flicked it open and began to read aloud from chapter 19, the crucifixion.

Every so often he would pause and say, *"Hawh!"* or *"Hawh-awh!"* As he read I prayed that something of the story would touch him. Suddenly, his voice faltered. Fat tears began to run down his cheeks. Hastily he rose and thrust yen notes at me.

"No," I said. "Please take it. It's free."

It took two and a half hours of hard climbing to make my way back to Karuizawa the following day. Along the route I prayed for that policeman. Even today I often pray for him – an ordinary man, custodian of an insignificant Japanese village on an out-of-the-way hillside, who read the story of the crucifixion for the first time and was overwhelmed by the love of God.

In the summer vacation I took another trip out into the surrounding district. On one occasion I was on a train, surrounded by a group of people I had met in another town. They had been attending a glider club meeting. They found it difficult to understand that I had boarded the train with little idea of where I would get off. To alleviate their confusion, I told them I was heading for a small market town called Naganohara. It was evening when I arrived and wearily made my way to a hotel opposite the station.

"No rooms," I was told.

I had never been turned away from a hotel or guest house before, but no amount of pleading would make the staff change their minds.

"No rooms," they insisted. "There is another inn at the other end of town."

Grudgingly, slighted by their abrupt refusal to find me a bed, I trudged away, increasingly aware of the burden of the heavy literature I was carrying. The town, a succession of farm houses, ran like a long ribbon alongside a river. The inn,

Eddie Metcalf (far right) with the tribal pioneers. Yunnan, 1911.

Steve being carried in a basket on the long journey from the provincial capital, Yunnanfu, to Taku, 1930.

Taku Village where Steve grew up. Yunnan, China, 1936.

Steve (right) with his Lisu friends – Xiao Yang is on the left. China, 1936.

Steve amongst the POWs liberated from the camp at Weifang. China, 1945.

The Metcalf family
(Steve, Ruth, Bessie,
Eddie) reunited in
Australia after the war,
1946.

Steve studying in Kanagi – one of his first placements in Japan, 1955.

Baptisms in Kanagi River. Japan, 1956.

Headmaster Fujita-san who walked through a blizzard to meet the missionaries after reading about them in the newspaper.

The Kanagi church group. When Steve and Don Morris started work in the area there were no believers. Steve is seated far right. Kanagi, Japan, 1955.

Steve handing out tracts on the streets of Goshogawara. Japan, 1950s.

Steve with the Boys' Bible Class. Goshogawara, 1956.

Steve and Evelyn on their wedding day. Japan, 3rd July 1957.

Evelyn teaching English in Otaru. Japan, 1969.

Steve and Evelyn in front of their snow-laden house in Aomori City, shortly before they returned to the UK. Japan, 1973.

Steve outside the old Metcalf home in Taku with the present owners. China, 2005.

which turned out to be a cheap, shabby establishment, seemed miles away. However, the greeting, when I finally lumbered through the doors, was friendly, and I was shown to a room with a rickety balcony.

Across the street was a store that sold everything from chopsticks to stove piping. It opened at five-thirty each morning and closed at eleven at night. The industrious proprietress was prepared to take literature from me, but she said that she would never find time to read it. In an upstairs window sat a man who played a little xylophone. He rarely moved from his seat and appeared to have some mental disability. It was a pathetic sight which seemed to draw me time and again during my stay.

I laid down on the straw mats and fell asleep. A petite maid, wearing a short apron tied at the waist over her elegant kimono, woke me with her laughter and told me that my bath was ready. All the baths I had seen before were wooden barrels. Here, a large copper cauldron standing over a fire dominated the pokey bathroom. Floating on the water was a wooden lid, which I carefully removed before easing myself into the hot water. I got out a good deal quicker! The hot copper had seared the skin off the soles of my feet. A little wiser, I replaced the wooden "lid" and let it sink beneath my feet.

If the mental image of a missionary in a cannibal's dinner-pot has not already suggested itself, it would be entirely appropriate. I emerged glad to be having a meal, not being the meal. The maid served me a dish of meat with a raw egg broken over it, a bowl of rice and the ubiquitous cup of tea. I think she found me amusing. She talked to me incessantly. While I nodded my understanding, I had not a clue what she was saying. Sleep, when I finally crawled beneath the shelter of a mosquito net, came very easily.

I was awakened by the maid turning on the light and announcing I had a visitor. In a formal greeting, a young man dressed in a kimono bowed low on the straw floor-mat. I tumbled groggily off my mattress and found sufficient balance to return the greeting politely. He handed me a visiting card but I couldn't read it. He then undid his cloth *furoshiki* and produced a New Testament in Japanese, two dictionaries and a number of other Japanese books. With no apparent embarrassment for disturbing my sleep, he opened the New Testament.

"Please," he indicated a page, "please teach me the meaning."

Suddenly my befuddled brain understood. This was what I had come to Japan to do. This was why I had been refused a room at the other hotel. This was why I had dragged my literature well over a mile all along that depressing street.

The maid reappeared with a tray and two cups of tea. The man produced a packet of Japanese *karinto* – miniature fried dough nuggets caked in brown sugar, which we nibbled at over the next two hours. I found my bilingual New Testament. By eleven o'clock my head swirled with Japanese words, most of which I had just dug out of the dictionary. Any hope that my earnest pupil was aware of the time was dashed with every new question. I felt incapable of finding another lucid expression or coherent phrase to satisfy his inquisitiveness.

"Perhaps I can pray," I suggested.

"Yes."

"Then I will sleep."

"I would like to pray also."

This was the first time, outside of my language classes,

114

that I had prayed in Japanese. When I had finished he remained sitting very still, eyes closed.

"You want to pray?" I asked.

He looked up in surprise. "You have finished?"

"Yes. 'Amen' means I have finished."

He nodded, picked up a pen and started to draw.

"This is Buddha," he explained. "Here... the Shinto gods. These are the *Hotoke* – the departed souls of people. This is Jesus Christ. Which god shall I pray to?"

Bleary-eyed, I turned to Acts chapter 17 – Paul's address to the men of Athens – and asked him to read while I prayed silently. At verse 23 he stopped.

"The God no one has seen? I don't know of him."

"Then read on."

A few moments later he stopped again and pointed to the picture he had drawn.

"Buddha and all these gods are made with hands. But this God doesn't live in temples made with hands. He is the great Creator. All things have life from him... Now he commands all men everywhere to repent." This new understanding was evident in his face. "I will pray to the true God," he said. "The God whom I do not know."

Downstairs the clock struck twelve.

Around five, I was awakened by the same sincere young man calling up to me from the street. He was off to work. He cheerily waved the booklet "Here is the Way" I had given him. At breakfast I asked the maid what his name was.

"Ma–su–da," she said slowly, for my benefit. She pointed out a farmhouse just across the street. The supplementary string of words that she followed up with may well have been his whole family history, but I was no wiser from one end to the other. Over the next couple of days I learned more about Masuda-san. He was twenty-eight, unmarried and a farmer. It was his elder brother I had seen in the room above the shop. His sad condition was the result of an accident. Masuda now had to provide for him and the family. He was a member of the town committee for religious festivals and responsible for the area's shrines.

I took him to the church, a warm-hearted congregation of around fifteen that appeared to consist mainly of one extended family and had not had a pastor for twenty years. I asked them to provide him with teaching. A fortnight later Masuda sat next to a blind man, whose dedication to Christ, despite his disability, really impressed him. Masuda was moved to tears by the hymns.

After that, Masuda wrote to me regularly. He was going to church. He had asked for an application form to become a Christian! He was telling everyone that 8 August, the day we met, was his spiritual birthday. He was having trouble with family and friends. The Festival and Shrine Committee were not happy with his new faith.

He had no lack of questions. Who were the Pharisees? Where is Gehenna? Were Roman Catholics Christians? Where does it mention Christmas trees in the Bible? The Bible talks about the children of God, but God only had one Son – what does this mean? What is baptism?

He had noticed that I didn't go to pinball parlours, nor did I play Japanese chess or gamble. I gave money to the church and the poor. At night I didn't want to sleep with girls.

"I had an image of foreigners living in luxury. Foreigners despicably chewing gum. Images of foreigners sitting in smoke-filled rooms drinking heavily. Only eating bread and butter and cheese, rejecting to eat rice meals…" he wrote. I was his model of Christian living. He had talked to the maid at the inn to find out more about me. As a result he had given up smoking and drinking Japanese wine. He had cut out snacks between meals. He had given up singing bawdy songs and was singing hymns. His favourite hymn was "My latest sun is sinking fast"[27] – a song usually sung at funerals!

Masuda was the first Japanese I helped to become a Christian. The people in the church said it was an act of God that he went to the inn to visit me. Given my lack of grace and the paucity of my Japanese that evening, I can only agree with their conclusion.

遠路
Enro
(Long Road)

In February 1951, when the China Inland Mission was losing its mandate for mission, Bishop Frank Houghton, the General Director, was in Melbourne. The Mission, he wrote, must "go forward into the mists of uncertainty". With the withdrawal of missionaries from Yunnan to Shaanxi and from Xining to Shanghai, there was doubt whether any of them could return to work in China. Houghton, my mentor, Oswald Sanders, and other leaders of the mission spent two days in prayer and five in conference. They emerged from their consultation with an exciting and compelling consensus revealed in a telegram to the home countries and Hong Kong: "Lengthen cords, strengthen stakes... from Thailand to Japan". The Mission would pursue its work amongst Chinese in other Asian countries, praying that in time work in China would be re-established. Surveys of several countries, including Indonesia, Malaya, the Philippines and Thailand were to be carried out to determine where missionaries could best be deployed.

Japan had little claim on the mission's attention and was an odd addition to the list. Houghton described the decision to include Japan: "some of us felt that instead of crossing a stream on clearly marked stepping-stones, we were being asked to make a leap forward into the stream itself! Or was

118

there a stepping stone?" Their final resolution was confirmed by the remarkable contents of that morning's post. With God-given timing, a friend of the mission was donating £500, half to aid the evacuation of China, half for new work in Japan. Another letter brought a second donation. Sudan Interior Mission had been given a cheque for $1,000 earmarked for mission in Japan. They were unable to use the gift – would CIM be willing to take it?

By May 1951 a three-man survey team to Japan had completed their work, the property at Karuizawa had been secured for language students, and candidates, myself among them, were coming forward to serve on the new field. Leonard Street, a former China hand, was designated to head up the work. Expansion into Japan, under the new name of the Overseas Missionary Fellowship, was rapid. The first phase of outreach from the base at Karuizawa came in 1952 when OMF missionaries were sent to seven centres on the northern island, Hokkaido.

If I needed any personal confirmation of my decision to go to Japan, the revival in Karuizawa at New Year 1953 was more than a stepping stone. I was asleep in my room when shouting in the corridor outside woke me. I looked bleary-eyed at Doug and he trudged over to open the door.

"Revival has broken out! Revival has broken out!" It was Jim, who slept next door to us.

"Er..."

"The TEAM missionaries have been praying for finance."

"Right..."

OMF shared the language facility with The Evangelical Alliance Mission. They had about a hundred missionaries prepared to move into new ministries, but lacked sufficient funds for the work.

"This evening someone got up and said that if they wanted God to move other people to give, they needed to put their hands in their own pockets first," Jim explained.

The response was dramatic. People were confessing their sin and, one after another, standing up to offer cash, cars and jewellery. These events were likened to the Macedonian Church, who "out of the most severe trial, their overflowing joy and their extreme poverty welled up in rich generosity… they gave as much as they were able, and even beyond their ability."[28]

In the evenings that followed I joined the TEAM prayer meetings, where scores of young missionaries poured out their hearts in prayer for the evangelization of Japan. I witnessed healing of relationships. Many missionaries found interpreters and went out preaching. There were numerous conversions. Whilst, in the period immediately after this event, we had perhaps our greatest response from Japanese to our outreach, I also believe that this revival in the missionary community was God's preparation of his people for the many years of perseverance that lay ahead of us. It was a most refreshing spiritual experience. I was caught up in a renewed vision to see Japanese turn to Jesus. I was eager to complete my language studies and get to work with the people I had come to serve.

In May 1954 I was asked to travel north to meet Leonard Street and his interpreter, Ono-san. They were travelling south from Hokkaido. We met at the ticket barrier at Aomori railway station. In the war 90 per cent of Aomori City had been destroyed by bombing and the rebuilding programme was not yet complete. The poorer sections of society still occupied temporary barracks. Their situation contrasted sharply with other Japanese who had taken advantage of the rapid recovery of the national economy on the back of the Korean War. In the better shops washing machines, refrigerators, radios, even TVs, were on sale for those who could afford them. Leonard Street, Ono-san and I were about to embark on a three-week survey of Aomori Prefecture.

Our first stop was the town of Goshogawara, an hour's journey away on a bus which lacked padded seats. The concrete road was so badly damaged that it was more comfortable to stand. The route took us through the region's famous apple orchards, heading west before breasting the crest of a hill at the base of the Tsugaru Peninsula. The views were spectacular. The panorama to the south was dominated by a stunning three-peaked volcano, Mount Iwaki, crested with snow. A ridge of hills ran north to a natural harbour shaped like a ray fish, its long river-tail flexing towards us down the length of the plain. In front of us was a pleasing pattern of rectangular rice fields, the landscape dotted here and there with small villages. At its centre lay Goshogawara, which means "five places river plain".

The church at Goshogawara had been a tobacco factory. There was a congregation of around forty. The pastor, one of only sixteen Japanese ministers in the Aomori Prefecture, was the son of a war widow, a woman of "ill repute". At a street meeting he had heard a Japanese preacher speak of the woman caught in adultery and had been drawn to faith in Jesus through his words, "He that is without sin among you, let him first cast a stone at her."[29]

"Missionaries are very rich," he told us. "The people cannot relate to them. You will need to break down barriers.

121

There is intolerance. There will be prejudice."

From there we headed north to Kanagi, a smaller town at the foot of the hills, with a river running through it; it was home to 9,000 people. The place derived its wealth from local cedar-wood and was known for its trade in black-market *sake*. It had also become a centre for dark magic.

Our third destination was Hirosaki, one of the impressive old cities of Japan, standing guard at the southern end of the Tsugaru Plain in the shadow of Mount Iwaki. The city was famous for its annual cherry-blossom festivals in the grounds of an elegant, three-tiered, white castle constructed in the seventeenth century. We were welcomed by a female pastor. She said she had been praying for missionaries to come and work in the area. A national leader of her denomination had written a book about a movement which would take the gospel back to Jerusalem from Japan. The concept of conquering lands from east to west had attracted the attention of Japan's military strategists. Regrettably, the vision of Jesus ruling, rather than the Emperor, smacked of sedition, and the church leaders were imprisoned and their churches were closed. As a result this Hirosaki church had been decimated.

In time I would work in all three of these places – Goshogawara, Kanagi and Hirosaki – but for the moment we retraced our steps to Aomori City to seek the advice of some of the ten missionaries from other missions already at work in the region. Perhaps the greatest need for the gospel, they told us, was amongst the fishing families who lived on the fringes of the Tsugaru Plain, many residing in coves and inlets inaccessible for three months of the winter, save by sea; places where the unfamiliar dialects of Aomori Prefecture were the common language.

Leonard Street and Ono-san left me to complete the survey myself. For another three weeks I bumped along in buses over tracks and trails and stayed at pokey inns. In places the bus could go no further and I was forced to walk.

"How far is it to the next village?" I asked a local man.

"You'll need five straw sandals," he replied.

I looked at him blankly. "Five sandals?"

"Two for your feet, two for your hands and one for your nose to climb the cliffs."

He and the crowd that had gathered burst into laughter. Japanese humour was lost on me. I found myself on a regular diet of dried fish and seaweed – it left a lot to be desired. In fact, until I learned to convey the fact that omelettes were nice, all the food seemed to taste of fish.

The town of Imabetsu on the north coast, now the entrance to the rail tunnel to Hokkaido Island, was one of the many that I visited. I booked into yet another inn and "tucked into" another dish of dried fish, seaweed with rice and raw eggs. A young man, about my age, approached me holding a Bible.

"I am the innkeeper's son," he said. "I work in the Post Office."

"Please." I invited him to sit down.

He was keen to tell me his story. My seaweed could wait.

"When I was younger I had TB," he said. "I went to a sanatorium. I learned about Jesus. From then on I always wanted to believe in him. There is so much I do not understand. But nobody can teach me. I have no one to pray with. I can never sing hymns. I am the only one interested here."

"Why have you come to me?" I was puzzled. Did it seem so obvious I was a Christian?

"Your name is Sutepano. I saw it in the guest book. I have read the story of Sutepano in my Bible. You are a missionary. You can teach me the truth."

He was right. I was named after Stephen, whose story he had found in Acts 6 and 7. My father had been translating that passage into Eastern Lisu when I was born. I was a missionary. And I could teach him the truth.

Later, as I left him and Imabetsu behind, I was struck by the fact that there were few large villages along the coast, yet the shoreline was studded with shacks, one after another, home after home, as far as the eye could see. I was moved by the plight of these people. There were thousands of fishermen and their families, caught up in ancestral cults and customs, who were denied the opportunity to learn the truth about Christ.

During my travels I encountered a reticence amongst the Japanese to talk about the war. The subject was taboo. It was the same wherever you went in Japan, I was told, not just because my Japanese was still very basic. In the mid fifties many Japanese were still rebuilding their lives; the occupation of foreign administrators and forces was barely over.[30] But, even when my language ability improved to a level capable of understanding, the subject was rarely raised. The silence had roots deep in the culture of the country and, as a consequence, lasted much longer than may have been expected. It was not until Hirohito, the Emperor, died, that I found people felt at liberty to express their opinions.

I returned to Karuizawa with a renewed vigour for my language studies. I needed to be well prepared for my first placement. The mission now had twenty-eight workers on Hokkaido and another fifteen, including myself, in language study at Karuizawa. Although we had already commenced church-planting ministries and were trying to work with Japanese churches, it was clear that we had no one who could yet speak and understand Japanese adequately. At our June field conference I gave my report on my trip to Aomori Prefecture. The learning of a new dialect was too much of a challenge, I told them; we needed to consolidate our language programme first.

Despite this, I was informed that the decision had already been made. I would go to Aomori City for four months, where Don Morris, a new Canadian worker, would join me, and in October the two of us would start a new work in Kanagi.

逆風
Gyakufuu
(Adverse Wind)

In Aomori City my father's foresight about OMF's early policies in Japan proved correct, and I was taught important lessons about sensitivity to the views of Japanese Christians. The mission's policies and practices had been hammered out through decades of determined ministry in China, often through hardship and grave circumstances. Added to this, in the 1950s, it was atheistic communism, not religious fundamentalism, that the West feared. In Japan we could not buy property, lest we lose it to another China-style revolution. Limited records should be kept, because nationals needed to be protected if OMF were forced to leave. For the same reason, Japanese should not be employed. With a perception of having "little time" in which to work, the mission lacked a long-term vision. One Japanese pastor commended OMF for their evangelistic zeal in the first years of work in Japan, but astutely noted that they had no understanding of the Japanese church. In hindsight such an approach seems ill conceived. But, at the time, the aggressive rise of atheism in Asia was a factor that few, if any, could see beyond.

Transferring policies used in China to another culture was often naive, occasionally disastrous. I was acutely aware of my lack of language ability, but the rules dictated that I must not preach by interpretation lest I became dependent on it. I spent hours working my way through every last syllable of a sermon with a university student, until he finally plucked up courage to say that he could interpret for me. I refused and ploughed on. It was a stalwart effort, no doubt, but the congregation at the little Baptist church in Aomori City to which I had attached myself were less than impressed with the bumbler who wanted to be their pastor. They were too polite to say so, of course.

The disenchantment of the group deepened when Don and I moved on to Kanagi just eight weeks later. Our replacements, a couple from Canada, had even less language than us. They too only stayed a few months before moving on. Then, a young disabled Japanese man and his wife, under the guidance of a mature OMF missionary, were given the leadership and there was a period of growth. But when the Japanese pastor left for Bible School training, the church was disbanded. Unfortunately, a number of the members and seekers stopped going to church.

"The missionaries are always changing. And they can't speak Japanese," was the complaint I frequently heard. This had been my first church in Japan and, although my stay had been short, I had grown attached to the congregation. Often I would lay awake at night reflecting how our lack of competence in language, poor placement policy and a strategy of not allowing interpretation had created this sad situation.

In Kanagi Don and I had trouble finding accommodation. In the end we rented three rooms above a sewing school. There was no running water and the toilets were out the back. We had to go to the public baths and draw water from a well at the bottom of the stairs. The rooms were measured according to the number of *tatami* – straw mats measuring two metres by

127

one metre – laid out on the floor. We had two ten-mat rooms and a six-mat living-room, plus a kitchen where we cooked on a charcoal brazier. The flat was divided by four striking hand-painted paper sliding doors, cherry blossom adorning one side and carp the other. When the need arose we could remove these doors completely and enjoy the space of a twenty-six-mat room.

The day after we arrived was Sunday and we arranged for our two nineteen-year-old neighbours – a laundry-man, Kakuta-san, and a farmer – to come for Bible study that evening. Their arrival coincided with torrential rain.

"Typhoon," said Kakuta. "It will be a big one."

We lowered the window shutters to keep out the worst of the weather and tried to teach them a hymn and read the Bible, while our building swayed back and forth, creaking and shuddering under the battering of a typhoon. The lights went out. Don found some candles and we carried on regardless. Finally, the two men thanked us, purchased the New Testaments we offered them and ran home through the storm. The typhoon did a great deal of damage. We suffered no more than losing our back door, but five ferries sank in the Tsugaru Strait with the loss of 1,430 people, among them an American missionary, Dean Leeper, who gave his life-jacket to another passenger.[31]

Kakuta showed real interest in the gospel and read the entire New Testament five times in three weeks. Six months later he was baptized along with another young man, a photographer. Kakuta was an excellent witness to his friends. Among them was Koya Kawamura, who worked in a bookshop and subsequently became a highly regarded pastor. Sadly, a couple of years later, Kakuta ran up horrific debts through gambling and fled to Yokohama City. It was forty-five years before I received more news of him. A German missionary told me that Kakuta was dying of cancer. Aware that he would not live long, Kakuta had walked into a church announcing that he wanted to pray and sing hymns. He regained his faith and his wife and children started going to church as well.

Another man who took many years to make a true commitment was a headmaster who lived in a village some three hours' walk away. Fujita-san and a Christian friend had read an article in the newspaper about the missionaries in Kanagi and walked through a snow blizzard in order to meet us. Fujita was keen for us to come to his school.

There was another blizzard the day we visited. Unable to see the road ahead, I kept my head down, and so walked right into something – the back end of a farm horse! Fortunately the horse didn't react to this assault on its "person" and kept its huge hooves on the ground. We settled ourselves in Fujita's living-room and he explained why he had asked us to come.

"Japan has changed. The war changed everything. I am too old to give up the gods, but our children must become Christians."

I pointed out the shrine that stood in the corner of the room. "If you die worshipping the ancestral spirits, then your children will be expected to worship you. They will believe that your spirit remains here, not returning to the true God."

Fujita listened and sat for a while, pondering what I had said.

"I understand," he said at last. "I understand. I will become a seeker of the Christian way."

It took twenty years for him to find his way to Christ. A Christian insurance salesman contacted me when I was living in Aomori City. Fujita-san was one of his customers and wanted to study the Bible with me again. Our friendship was renewed. I kept in regular contact until his daughter phoned to say that Fujita had fallen down a flight of stairs. He was in the hospital, paralysed from the waist down, with acute pain in his abdomen caused by a damaged nerve in his spine.

"Is it too late to become a Christian?" he asked.

I read the Bible and he made a profession of faith. A few weeks later he died. His family gave him a Buddhist funeral and then we had a special service at the church. His son thanked us publicly. They found the expensive Buddhist ceremonies an array of confusing chants, something akin to journeying through a dark tunnel. In the church they said they had emerged into the light. They knew their father was with Jesus. Later, the son became a Christian himself.

If our Japanese skills were at times inadequate, our knowledge of the local dialect was negligible. On one occasion a retired Japanese came to see us. His navy-blue suit was a little too tight for him and was well worn along the seams. He made himself comfortable on our living-room *tatami* and launched into his story. I had no clue what he was talking about. I looked at Don. He looked at me.

"I'll make tea," said Don.

He disappeared in the direction of the kitchen, returned briefly with a round tray bearing our small teapot, two handleless cups and a porcelain plate with biscuits, put it on the low table between my guest and me, and then rapidly disappeared again. I let the tea draw and handed a cup to the man on a wooden saucer. He gracefully inclined his head by way of thanks.

The reprieve from his monologue was brief; he was

soon in full flow once more. I leaned forward in an attempt to sift out any words I understood, straining for anything that would give some sense to his conversation. I found his tale simply unintelligible. Nothing stemmed the flood of incomprehensible phrases. For about an hour I knelt opposite him until my legs and brain could take no more.

"Please excuse me, Sensei,"[32] I said as he paused momentarily to sip his tea.

The man nodded slightly. I bowed, slid open the paper doors and escaped.

"Don!" I nodded towards the living-room. "You have a turn. I'm worn out."

He took my place and the man surged on. I listened with amusement through the paper doors to Don's confident interjections: "Is that so…?", "Really?" His pretended aplomb did not last.

"Go back in," he told me. He was grim faced. He had survived no more than twenty minutes. "I haven't understood a word. Not a single word," he said.

Our guest could not be left alone. Reluctantly I knelt opposite him again and submitted once more to his deluge of words. It was three quarters of an hour before the man dried up. He pulled a watch on a chain from his waistcoat pocket, inspected the timepiece carefully, replaced it, wrapped the remaining biscuits in some tissue paper and indicated he must leave. There was a great deal of bowing before we, thankfully, escorted him downstairs to the door.

Don and I arranged for a number of groups to visit our home for Bible study. Among them were the girls from the sewing school downstairs. One Monday morning they arrived to find one of their number slumped in a cupboard. She was

131

dead. She had taken five packets of sleeping tablets. In her hand was a note – "Life is tranquil. I am slowly getting sleepy. Upstairs they are singing beautiful hymns. What a lovely atmosphere to make my exit from life."

This shocking episode brought home to me the reality of the Japanese problem of suicide. The act was seen as an honourable way to escape from problems or personal shame. Thousands of Japan's soldiers killed themselves rather than be captured by the Allies. High-school children took their own lives as a solution to the stresses that school work imposed. Disgraced politicians died in the same manner. Even today suicide remains a real issue in Japan. In 2007 the Japanese government produced a white paper in an attempt to address the problem. Suicide rates are higher than 30,000 per year – more than 90 per day. I began to realize that every Japanese person I knew had some acquaintance, family member or friend who had committed suicide.

Some time later I preached on the fact that our lives belong to God. "Suicide is akin to rebellion against God," I said. "It is self-murder." The following week a school teacher told me that one of her friends at the meeting had been determined to die. After the service she went to lie out in the snow, waiting for the cold to kill her. My message came back to her, challenging her decision. She struggled to her feet and found her way home. She was resolved to live, because it was God alone who should decide when her life would end.

In the spring of 1955 Don married and relocated to Hokkaido, leaving me to work in Kanagi alone. I hoped to have a new worker join me, but the field council decided I was to move on again, this time to Goshogawara. "You are good at starting new work," they told me, though Kanagi was the only "new work" I had started. My Australian Director, Oswald Sanders, gave me good support and remonstrated with the council, saying that such a move would destabilize the work Don and I had done. The council were adamant; they had prayed and made a unanimous decision. That was the end of the matter. Regrettably, Sanders was proved right and the work in Kanagi did suffer as a result.

However, our brief ministry in Kanagi was not ineffective. In 1960 the Goshogawara church had the distinction of appointing the first Japanese pastor to come forward through our ministry. This was none other than Koya Kawamura from our fellowship at Kanagi, who had become a Christian through the witness of Kakuta, our laundry-man.

Before that, however, I was to suffer personal loss. In January 1956, my dad passed away.

哀歌
Aika
(Song of Lament)

My father was born in Warstone Lane, close to Birmingham's Jewellery Quarter, on 3 March 1879, the third of four sons for Samuel and Emma Metcalf. My grandparents ran both a jeweller's and a greengrocer's store. They must have been reasonably wealthy because they were able to hire a servant girl. The eldest son, Joe, took over the family businesses and opened a kiosk selling fruit at Birmingham New Street railway station. John, who became an accountant, went deaf at the age of twelve as a result of measles. Arnold, the youngest of the four, was closest to my father and became a minister in the Methodist Church. Christened George Edgar, my father was known as "Eddie", except by my mother who always called him Edgar.

Eddie, Joe and Arnold were converted in their late teens. Out on a Sunday stroll, they were drawn into a crowd listening to the Revd Dr Frederick Luke Wiseman, a biographer of Charles Wesley, preaching in the open air. Although the family were nominally Baptists, Wiseman's influence led the three sons to join the Methodist Church and all became local preachers.

Eddie took an apprenticeship in tailoring and for a while had his own shop in Oxford. His training stood him in good stead in China, where he could still cut himself a fine suit when the occasion demanded. Before the 1911 revolution, however, he regularly wore Chinese gowns and grew a queue in local fashion. This lengthy plait of dark-brown hair he eventually cut off, depositing it in a cocoa tin. It was an item of immense intrigue for me as a child.

If my experiences in Japanese POW camp were instrumental in taking me to Japan, it was another conflict forty-five years earlier which had stirred my father to serve in China. In 1900 the Boxer Rebellion wreaked havoc with missionary efforts in north China. On New Year's Eve an English missionary working with the Society for the Propagation of the Gospel in Foreign Parts[33] in Shandong Province, the Revd Sidney Brooks, was set upon by thirty armed men and decapitated. He was the first missionary martyr of the uprising. This tragic incident marked the beginning of the Boxers' brutal persecution of Christians, both Chinese and foreign. Before foreign armies laid siege to Beijing and brought the conflict to an end, more than 180 Protestant missionaries, including over 50 children, had been killed, alongside nearly 2,000 Chinese believers. An estimated 30,000 Chinese Roman Catholics and around 40 of their foreign workers were also murdered.

It was in response to these horrific stories of martyrdom and the apparent plight of the unevangelized Chinese that my father offered to join the China Inland Mission, the organization that had suffered the majority of the missionary losses. Wiseman was an admirer of James Hudson Taylor and CIM, but he had doubts about Eddie's ability to learn Mandarin. Eddie was adamant in his reply: "If God has called me, God will equip me to do the work he has called me to."

Wiseman was firmly reminded of God's words to Moses: "Who gave this man his mouth? Who makes him deaf or mute? Is it not I, the Lord? Now go; I will help you speak and will teach you what to say."[34]

Wiseman, wisely, raised no further objections. Eddie was admitted to the CIM training home at Newington Green in London and spent some time in basic medical instruction at the Mildmay Hospital. He sailed for China on 14 September 1906, arriving over five weeks later in Shanghai, where he adopted the Chinese name Wang Huairen (Cherish Benevolence)[35] and began his studies.

I always remember my father as a quiet man with a strong determination for detail. He applied these qualities to his Mandarin study in Nanjing, vying for top place in the exams and, despite his pastor's reservations, gaining a reputation for his language abilities. The mission designated Eddie to ministry in south-west China. It took Eddie nine months to complete the thousand-mile journey, on horseback or by boat, where possible, and walking the rest of the way.

Eddie was assigned to work with three minority groups, the Eastern Lisu, the Laka and the Dai. Few of these far-flung tribes spoke Mandarin and he embarked on learning new languages, finally adopting the homelands of the Eastern Lisu as his own. Using his talents on the trumpet and concertina to accompany the hymns he knew and those he wrote, he trekked miles across the mountains in search of new villages and unreached Lisu, proclaiming the message of salvation. At Taku he established a Bible School to teach native pastors and evangelists.

For many years Eddie chose not to marry, believing that the remoteness and deprivation of his situation was no place for a woman. Perhaps the loneliness engendered by singleness or the pressures created by the marriages of his colleagues changed his mind. But I like to think that it was the eye-catching appearance of Elizabeth Mary Donnelly in the missionary circles of Yunnan that swept aside his old-fashioned male doughtiness. Certainly their short courtship proves that Eddie did not wait long to propose to my mother. They were married at the British Consulate General in Kunming on 19 January 1921, her thirtieth birthday. He was forty-one.

Bessie, as my mother was always called, was the daughter of a florist in Adelaide and granddaughter to emigrants from Ireland and Scotland. She had a love of literature, was trained in elocution and had acquired a beautiful accent. She arrived in China on 28 November 1917, eleven years after my father, but I was told that she proved a better Lisu speaker than him. I have vivid pictures of her perpetual busyness. Aided by servants in the daily chores of a labour-intensive existence, she gathered together groups of native women and provided them with Bible teaching. On her retirement she had a reputation as a good speaker and was frequently invited to meetings to share her experiences of China.

Eddie and Bessie established their home at Taku and swiftly learned that their few possessions were attractive to bandits. After having their home ransacked three times in quick succession, they determined to live as simply as possible. Eddie was taken hostage on a number of occasions. During the brief spell after the war when we were living together in Melbourne, my father and I would sit in a couple of chairs in the living-room and he would tell me his stories.

"There was the time Carl Gowman[36] and I got carted off with Evangelist Ma and a couple of Chinese school teachers. That was before your mother and I were married. Forty-odd brigands ransacked the house for every last clock, watch, knife, fork and spoon. Gowman escaped that evening. The teachers were released and then Ma made his escape. That was remarkable, you know. Each time the Lisu Christians gathered to pray, one of us got away.

"I was held for five days. Then my guard got lazy. He was taking me back to the loft where I was sleeping. At the corner of the house he turned right. I went left. I just walked off into the night. It was dark enough to slip away but not light enough to see where I was going. I fell down an embankment and got caught behind three small trees! I couldn't go forward and I definitely wasn't going back. So I was stuck there for several hours until the bandits called off the search. Even then, one of the clever devils stayed close, hiding a few feet from where I was wedged. If I'd moved, he would have caught me. Finally, he ran off and I was free to find my way to safety.[37]

"Now, did I ever tell you about the black-turbaned raiders in February '27? When Carpenter Yang was escaping with Ruth on his back and got shot at..."[38]

My dad had a down-to-earth response to foes and friends alike. He was there to serve them. He drew no distinction between the rogues and the righteous. All were welcome at his dispensary for medicine and treatment. I remember distinctly the theft of money from the clinic office one night. The thief had some days earlier made indiscreet inquiries about the strength of the wire-netting window-screens! Needless to say, the man was quickly apprehended, trussed up so tightly that the binding cut into his flesh, and dumped in front of my father for judgment. Squatting down, Eddie cut the thief's bonds to relieve his suffering.

"You can pay back when you're able," Eddie told him. "I have forgiven you, just as Christ has forgiven you."

The man was converted and baptized. I was six at the time, and such obvious lessons in forgiveness as this had a profound effect on my understanding of the power of reconciliation.

Eddie returned to Britain just twice to see his family. In 1917 his ship dodged German U-boats to make a safe passage home. He returned again in 1934 with Bessie, having left me with Ruth at Chefoo School. Visits to Australia to visit Bessie's family were equally infrequent – once in 1926 and then not again until the end of World War II, when he was due to retire.

Inevitably, as he grew older, my father had to review his ministry. By the late 1930s he lacked the energy to tackle the hardships of itinerant ministry in the mountains. A broken leg, sustained in a horse-riding accident, also caused him to reassess his strategy. He concluded he could better use his final years of missionary service by providing an enduring aid for the Lisu church, and devoted his time to Bible translation. With his meticulous care for words and meaning, he painstakingly composed his translation, constantly praying for inspiration when his lack of knowledge hampered progress. He found an Eastern Lisu word for "glory"[39] – *the gold of heaven* – in a sunset, and an expression for "comforter"[40] – *turn the corner more easily* – at a funeral.

By 1947 the ongoing struggle between the Communists and the Nationalist government in China was a concern. Yunnan remained within the control of the government, but the trials of Japanese occupation and an inflationary economy had sapped the strength of its army. However, my dad was anxious to finish the work and postponed his retirement in Australia to return to Taku.

Four years later Eddie and a team of church leaders completed their work on the New Testament, and a second hand-written copy was made. Yunnan had ceded to the Communist forces and mission agencies were reluctantly instructing their workers to leave. Eddie and Bessie made a distressing final journey to Hong Kong. Time and again the precious original was handed over for inspection, but always returned. At one bus station a young enthusiast for revolution, seeking to brand my father as a spy, grabbed the manuscript and held it aloft in triumph.

"See!" he yelled to the gathering crowd. "See! Proof of the old man's imperialist activities." He thrust his face into Eddie's. "How long have you been in China?"

My father took his question calmly. "Forty-five years. How long have you been in China?"

The joke was not lost on the crowd and their laughter forced the young man to lose face. Angrily he slung the manuscript into the mud and stalked away. Eddie scooped it up and carried it on to Hong Kong, where it was printed. Dozens of copies were posted into China, but none reached their destination. The copy in Yunnan remained hidden and then was lost during the long years of the persecution of the church. In 1999 my sister sent my father's original, complete with his corrections and hand-written notes, to China.

On their return to Adelaide, Eddie and Bessie were asked to act as CIM representatives in South Australia until my father retired in March 1955, just short of fifty years' service. His retirement at the mission bungalow, Cherith, in the Surrey Hills area of east Melbourne, was short-lived. I received a letter from him dated the end of November. The tone of his news was bright. He and my mother were enjoying a few days' holiday. With typical forthrightness he expressed his opinions on what he called the "spirit of Phariseeism" in the organization's old-fashioned policies – the ostracizing of young couples who wanted to get engaged in a manner that did not match the "hard and fast rules" of the mission.

His final letter, dated 8 January, arrived in Japan the day after his death – two sheets of paper written from the Royal Melbourne Hospital. The hand was weaker than his previous letters but still legible. He had been in hospital since the end of December with a blockage of the urinary tract, an illness that had claimed his brother Arnold's life just three months previously. He would undergo an operation the following morning. He hoped to be over the worst soon.

It was a procedure from which he never recovered. For a few days he had stood on the edge of eternity, weak and frequently in pain. "He was slipping away quickly," my mother wrote later. "I moistened his lips – he opened his eyes and seemed to know me – then they closed again – nobody came near, and an hour later he drew his last breath on earth and went in to see the King in His Beauty and to be changed into His likeness."

On Sunday, 15 January 1956, I was by myself at home in Kanagi, when the phone rang. The Japanese telegraphist politely read me the news from my mother. My father had passed away that afternoon. When the telegrapher finished she broke down into tears. I replaced the telephone receiver, my emotions in turmoil. I felt desperately alone.

At the funeral, held at Cherith, one of his junior co-workers spoke of Eddie's example, quoting a verse in 2 Timothy that best described my father: "Endure hardness as a good soldier of Jesus Christ."[41] He spoke of the "kinds of hardness of which

Eddie never complained – sickness, brigands, loneliness, hard journeys, coarse food etc. – all of which he accepted that he might win souls as a good soldier of Jesus Christ."

Eddie left nothing. He had "no bank account, no property, or possessions of any kind", another letter from my mother informed me; "Just his simple clothing & a few books. He laid up all his treasure in heaven."

Neither Ruth nor I were able to say our farewells to my father. Mine had taken place at Melbourne railway station as I left for Japan in 1952. As the train began to pull away, I looked for him amongst the crowd of well-wishers and thought I had missed him. He was standing alone, right at the tip of the platform. Waiting for me. Waiting to wave his goodbyes. It seemed important that we should have that final fleeting moment together.

Ruth, as matron of Cherith, looked after my mother until her death in August 1966. It was typical of my parents that I should, as I had from my dad, receive Bessie's final letter after the news of the heart attacks that killed her. My mother had faithfully written to me for thirty-two years, even through the long separation of the war years when none of her letters arrived.

In completing this part of my story, I want to quote my mother's words at a women's meeting in Berri. "It breaks my heart to say goodbye to my children. However, some people only have their children in this world; we have ours for all eternity." It will perhaps help you to understand the cost of missionary service for Eddie and Bessie, and the unfaltering hope that allowed them to meet all its challenges.

愛

Ai
(Love)

"Steve, a word?"

One of the married missionaries at the Karuizawa language course called me into his room. My senior colleague was obviously not at ease over something.

"Why are you... Well, why are you stringing one of our young ladies along?"

I looked at him in puzzlement.

"I think she deserves a little more respect."

"I'm not sure..."

"You need to bring it out in the open."

He paused, waiting for my answer. I can only think my expression was not confused enough for him to notice my bewilderment.

"It's not right, Steve. Not the way I'd expect you to be carrying on."

"Er...?"

"Everyone can see what's happening. In fact the matter is descending to the level of gossip. Never a good thing."

I was glad everybody was aware of the matter, because, whatever it was I was being accused of, it was certainly news to me.

"Who... who is it?" My question, though honest, sounded impudent.

"Steve, please don't play games with me."

"No, truthfully, I don't have a clue. Who are you talking about?"

His embarrassment was plain and I was not making his task any easier.

"Alice."

"Alice!"

"Yes, she has spoken to Jessie. Jessie has spoken to my wife. She has spoken to me and now I'm speaking to you."

I couldn't begin to fathom how in the world Alice had imagined I had any intentions towards her, but unmistakably something had gone truly awry.

"But she is ten... twelve years older than me," I argued. "Do you think it's... it's feasible?" A bad choice of word!

"What's wrong with that?"

"Well... well..." I spluttered. My colleague didn't look as though any argument was going to retrieve my reputation. "I'll go and see Jessie," I said.

Jessie proved less embarrassed, but was disappointed for Alice.

"I'm not even looking for a girlfriend, let alone a wife," I told Jessie.

"Some of the things you have said... Alice is convinced they were an indication..."

"She's mistaken. I'm very sorry, but she has misunderstood my intentions."

"She's not sleeping..."

"How long?"

"Months."

"Months!" I was horrified. My innocent conversations and actions had been keeping her awake at night. We were in

144

the same language class. We got on well enough. I had once been downtown and purchased a futon for her. I had asked her to take on an English class at a local High School because I had other commitments. I had invited her to help with the Sunday School. All inconsequential incidents as far as I was concerned. But not for her. We were the last two students in our year to be designated to our first ministries. Naturally we had talked about it. Perhaps we had talked for too long. Perhaps, perhaps...

Alice may have been mistaken, but according to missionary etiquette I was definitely to blame. I got quite angry before I offered to write to her and explain, as diplomatically as possible, the reality of the situation. It was four years before I received a reply – a measure, I think, of the depth of hurt Alice had experienced. I understood her feelings all too well. I had been there myself. But if my relationship with Joy had left me bereft, this incident left me baffled. I had loved Joy and my call to missionary work had separated us. Now I had unwittingly encouraged a missionary to lose herself to me. It was true that I had little interest in getting married but, undoubtedly, I needed to put my male brain into a different gear and learn to be sensitive to the females around me.

By the summer of 1956 I was settled at Goshogawara and increasingly aware that I could not manage the pastoral side of the work alone. I was twenty-eight and found myself mulling and praying over the prospects for marriage. Senior missionaries had dropped none-too-subtle hints about this female colleague or that, but I had not encountered anyone I considered attractive. I had regular contact with young Japanese women and there were a number of Japanese eager to arrange my marriage to some wealthy Japanese ladies! Under mission guidelines, however, any prospective Japanese wife would have to have Bible School training, or I would have to leave the mission. Added to this were my own feelings on the matter. In prison camp there had been a number of Eurasian families, and their experiences had left me with an unhelpful impression of what life was like for the children of mixed marriages.

At the evangelistic campaign in Hirosaki that summer I found the attractiveness of an energetic missionary from Ireland delightfully distracting. Evelyn Robinson was conspicuous in any setting, with her curls of lustrous red-brown hair. Her smile more than engaged me. And there was something about her large dark eyes that made me linger a little longer than I should. She had been studying Japanese in Aomori City for a year and a half (Karuizawa had been discontinued as the language school) and we had met briefly a few times before. When I was given the task of collecting a projector and other bits and pieces for our ministry, a six-hour round trip away, Evelyn, against her better judgment, was assigned as my assistant. As our bus trundled along under a scorching sun, she was cautious in conversation about herself and apparently didn't want to know anything about me. Feeling very awkward, I tried a new tack.

"Did you do any mission work before Japan?"

It proved a good move. She was enthusiastic about outreach in Scotland and her work with The Faith Mission. I was impressed. In fact, she was making all kinds of impressions on me that looked distinctly like an answer to my prayers.

There was little to indicate that any stirrings of affection were mutual. But, as is often the way of these things, I found it extremely difficult to get Evelyn out of my mind. I decided to write to her. I don't know what I expected but her reply was to the point: *No*.

Here I floundered on a dilemma. Evelyn's answer was unequivocal and I had no desire to invite further humiliation. On a deeper level, I could not escape from the fact that Evelyn was the person I wanted to share the rest of my life with. Three months later I risked more rejection with a second letter. Her reply was as strong and as concise as the first. She would be grateful if I did not pursue the matter any further. Her mind was made up. The response, nevertheless, did little to halt the intensity of my private turmoil. Of course, I prayed about it. I hadn't stopped praying since my visit to Hirosaki. I found myself hemmed in. Evelyn had become the sole owner of my affections. It even felt like a betrayal to consider anyone else. Yet the reality was that Evelyn's attitude was unambiguous. She was not interested in me. Full stop.

I buried myself in work. There were new seekers to attend to. I was running Bible studies for groups of young Japanese; all interested, all asking questions. As my language abilities had grown, I had become a more proficient preacher and I was in demand. I was travelling across the Prefecture to meetings. I had once preached to a congregation of over a thousand people. Frequently, at the end of a day, I would simply drop dead beat onto my mattress, exhausted with the day's busyness. TB was rife in the area and, as a regular visitor to hospitals, I was at risk. When I developed a rasping cough, David Hayman suggested I take a couple of days' break. We could go together to the Osorezan Mountains in north-east Honshu, where I could get the benefit of the sulphur pools. It sounded a good idea.

However, when we arrived we discovered the only

lodgings were in a Buddhist temple; cheaper than anything I had ever stayed in before but devoid of comfort. We endured the deprivations of plain food, a thin pillow, a complementary thin mattress and a room lacking any other furniture. No doubt the monks considered we were earning merit! Whilst I was getting in and out of steaming pools, set in pits of arid grey rock beneath leafless trees and filled with lurid yellow water that reeked of rotten eggs, David talked with the monks. The heavy congestion that had been strangling my breathing began to lift and we gratefully headed back to the bus stop. Unhappily, heavy rains had caused a landslide and it was another three days of frugal existence before a bus driver rescued us.

That winter I took a trip from Goshogawara to Aomori City with two female colleagues. Our train chugged out into a heavy snowfall, pushing on despite the increasingly difficult conditions. All along the track there were crews shovelling away the snow to aid our progress. Eventually we heaved to a halt at Kawabe junction, a siding of no more than twenty railwaymen's shacks used by local farmers to send their rice and apple crops to market. With no let up in the heavy snowfall, it was announced that the onward service to Aomori had been suspended and no trains would be risking the journey back to Goshogawara. We had the choice of standing on a snowbound platform or staying on the train, which was heading for Hirosaki.

For my companions there was only one option: we could visit the OMF missionaries in Hirosaki. I was less enthused about the prospect. Hirosaki was where Evelyn was now working. It had been four months since her second rejection and I had not seen her since. As our train struggled on through the blizzard, I began to think of dozens of reasons for avoiding the awkwardness of meeting.

A few hours later I sat in the porch of the mission home and pulled my boots off. Suddenly, a door to one of the bedrooms opened and out stepped Evelyn. She was as astounded to see me as I was embarrassed to be there.

"I need to have a word with you," she said. "I was praying earlier. I had a picture of your face and, no matter what, I couldn't get you out of my mind. In the end I told God that if he wanted me to marry you, I needed a sign. He would have to bring you here… this morning."

I was dumbstruck. God may move in very mysterious ways, but I am not sure he needed to bring the Japanese railway system to a halt to secure me a bride. Later that evening, as my companions and I travelled back to Goshogawara, they complained of the waste of a day. The drama that had unfolded for me was definitely worth every moment of our delay.

Evelyn and I arranged to meet in Hirosaki the following Monday – if it didn't snow! She had many questions, as you can well imagine. Who was this Australian with whom God had ambushed her? Apart from the understandable feelings any woman would have in marrying someone they hardly knew, I was not Evelyn's obvious choice of a partner. I was to all appearances a driven individual, scarcely stopping for holidays. She was barely over the initial language barrier and still dealing with culture shock. I had been raised in Asia and had a two-year start in Japan on her. She was three and a half years older.

Japanese culture did not allow for courtship. If we were to wed, then we must declare our intentions. We went ahead. We would marry in July – four months away. The date had

149

little to do with protocol or passion. It was simply when we would get our next allowance.[42] We would start our marriage with a little money in hand. I had £35 in the bank; enough to buy an engagement ring and a suit, and no more. Evelyn could borrow a wedding dress from an American friend.

We were married twice. First on 25 June 1957 in a legal ceremony at the British Consulate in Yokohama, an exhausting sixteen-hour train ride away; the express fare was just too expensive. In front of a few friends we completed the formalities, were taken out for a meal and then boarded the train back. If we were tired travelling south, we could barely keep our eyes open on the way home. The days that followed were endured, not enjoyed, as we waited for our church wedding. By now we were very much in love and couldn't bear tearing ourselves apart for another week.

A letter from our HQ in Singapore compounded our woe. Due to shortage of funds, it had been decided not to send out remittances. The money we were relying on would not be coming. We had no other recourse than prayer, and God did not disappoint us. Through the generous wedding gifts of our friends we were blessed with more money than OMF would have sent us. It was a salutary lesson in God's provision that neither of us has forgotten.

The wedding took place in the new chapel at Toogijuku Church College, Hirosaki. We posed for one or two coloured photos – then a great innovation – before we indulged in the opulence of strawberries and cream and were pampered by the generosity of flattering speeches. Unfortunately, one of our guests made off with our taxi to the railway station. Our train pulled out just before we scrambled onto the platform. My stunning new bride, wearing a going-away outfit sent from Britain, and her suitably spruce new husband ended up sitting on a very unromantic hard bench in the station waiting-room. There wouldn't be another train that night. My plans in disarray, we stayed in an uncomfortable inn for our first night as husband and wife. All I can say is that our honeymoon – a tour taking in a caldera lake, a hot-spring resort, a mountain plateau and finally a picturesque fishing village – more than made up for the hitch in our arrangements.

Five days later we returned to Goshogawara. It was evening and we stole quietly up the stairs to our apartment. Evelyn's possessions had arrived. Just a small locker box and a suitcase. In Japan the bride always brought furniture and her sizeable dowry. Our landlord must have shaken his head and wondered just who I had married. But it was enough. When Evelyn and I married, one Bible verse was quoted time and again on the cards we received: "For the Lord God is a sun and shield: the Lord will give grace and glory: no good thing will he withhold from them that walk uprightly."[43] Time and again we would learn that God was more than able to meet all our needs.

Our first child, Danny, was born in June 1958, followed by Philip and then John. When our daughter arrived in 1963 we gave her the name Elizabeth Margaret, a name that drew wry comment from our Japanese friends; they would never use royal names for their children. Convincing them that my mother was Elizabeth and Evelyn's mother was Margaret was not easy. Three years later we completed our family with the birth of James. Over the last fifty years our family has grown – to five families and ten grandchildren.

But before all that, Evelyn and I embarked on a new phase of ministry, working together amongst the people of Aomori Prefecture.

151

花開

Kaika
(Blossom)

The Matsuoka Hoyou-en Leprosarium, located on the west side of Aomori City, was home to around 700 leprosy patients. It was a pleasant site of narrow lanes running between orderly wooden buildings, with a lake and broad groves of woodland in the lee of the North Hakkoda Mountains. A very picturesque setting for the annual profusion of spring buds, the flowers smothering their trees with heavy mantles of pink-white blossom. Yet this beauty was of little consequence. The Japanese feared the place. While the disease itself had been tamed with drugs, the evidence of its debilitating damage was obvious to anyone who ventured inside the gates. There was nothing attractive about the scars etched into faces or the stubs of shortened limbs. But these people were loved by God. They were isolated, confined behind the walls of their compound, but God had not forgotten them.

Whilst Japan was at war, drugs were not available, and the number of deaths increased month on month. Among the patients was a tall Japanese named Kichi-san. The growing death toll moved him to intercede more earnestly for those around him without a faith in Christ. He began to fast and pray in a cornfield attached to the leprosarium. Then he recruited two women to join him. God worked a miracle, and in a couple of years the church had grown to over 100 believers.

Evelyn and I visited this leprosarium as often as was feasible from Goshogawara. Evelyn's ability as an organist was always welcome. The regular organist was the daughter of a local wealthy family who, on discovering she had leprosy, abandoned her at the institution's gates. With only three fingers and one thumb, she was still attempting to pound out a tune for the worship services. The church sang with great gusto and I have vivid memories of Kichi-san – his arms raised, hands with no fingers, his head without hair, his feet no more than stumps – praising God. Then he would kneel, shouting loudly, "Hallelujah! Hallelujah! Thank you, Father. Thank you I have leprosy. If I didn't have leprosy, I would never have been saved. Hallelujah!"

I also remember the day a young girl came to give her testimony. She was the daughter of a headmaster and one year had been selected as the city's beauty queen. Newly crowned, she was leaving the ceremony when a jealous competitor threw a bowl of sulphuric acid in her face. For months she lay in a Tokyo hospital ward, hiding her disfigured face from the world beneath her blankets, wanting to die. It was a Bible message on the radio that drew her back to life.

"Blessed are the pure in heart: for they shall see God."[44] The pastor explained, "Physical beauty is only skin deep. True beauty is found in the heart."

The girl asked for a New Testament and shortly afterwards became a Christian. Standing with the leprosy patients, she brought a real message of hope. Her face was a parable. One side was beautiful, the other an ugly mishmash of scarred tissue.

When she returned to Aomori she visited her rival.

"You meant it for evil," she explained to the girl, "but God meant it for good."

After Danny was born we took him with us to the leprosarium. A crowd of women formed around Evelyn. They had rarely seen a baby, they said. Children born in the compound were removed and no Japanese would dare bring an infant on a visit. Evelyn held out Danny to one of the women. She drew away. Evelyn persisted until the woman tentatively held out her two deformed hands and received our son. Tears streamed down her face. Evelyn's simple act spoke volumes for our faith, where thousands of words would have gone unheard. Our Christian friends at the leprosarium, however, were not just recipients of our help. At the beginning of each New Year they sent us a donation for our ministry. One Christmas we had been away for meetings and arrived home without a yen between us. The banks were closed, but a letter awaited us. It was a postal order from the church in the leprosarium, which could be cashed at the Post Office. It was one of the most humbling gifts I have ever received.

In the summer our main mode of evangelism was a series of tent missions conducted in the various towns around Aomori Prefecture. Some small events attracted an audience of just ten or twelve. Others, such as the April Cherry Blossom festivals, were fruitful opportunities to meet literally thousands of people. At other times we would simply go out onto the streets, attracting a circle of curious onlookers with a board and easel and a simple gospel message drawn out in characters.

At the Hirosaki Festival in 1956 over 450,000 tracts were given out by our team inside one week. The grounds around the castle were transformed into a circus of shrines, stalls selling everything from goldfish to tortoises, and cafés supplying snacks such as grilled fish on a stick and bags of chewy *surume* (dried, shredded cuttlefish). The walkways were decorated with colourful paper lanterns. A multitude of people streamed into the park. Children dressed in every shade of crimson and scarlet. School students in their navy-blue uniforms. Women, in formal kimonos and clogs, carrying babies on their backs. Farmers and fishermen in their rough work-clothes. Music groups set themselves up around the castle moat, beating out rhythms on *odaiko* and *otsuzumi* drums, plucking at thirteen-stringed zithers and three-stringed lutes or playing *takebue* bamboo flutes, while graceful dancers wove moving pictures of traditional tales. Sadly, the festival had also become an excuse for drinking parties to root themselves beneath the cherry blossom trees and drink *sake* until the company were well inebriated.

Our team of Japanese Christians and missionaries erected a tent by the river. It was my role to attract people to the meetings with a few tunes on my harmonica through a battery-operated speaker system. As the crowds clambered onto the wooden benches, we sang hymns and then one of the men gave a message. Special meetings were arranged for crowds of children who crammed in underneath the canvas. Sometimes we raised the sides of the tent to allow those standing or sitting outside to hear the message. Down at the gates six or eight members of the mission rapidly handed out tracts as fast as possible.

These tent missions were always hard work but earned us encouraging responses. Grandma Hisasue was one of those who attended a tent meeting in Goshogawara with her daughter and granddaughter. She was convinced that there was a god who heard her prayers. All during the war she had prayed for the safety of her eldest son, and he had returned home with three miraculous stories of being snatched away from what had seemed certain death. Twice he had been rescued when his ship had been sunk. On the third occasion he had slipped out of a dining-room to get a tray seconds before a bomb landed where he had been sitting. His comrades had been killed; only he had survived. As Grandma Hisasue listened to the evening messages she was convinced that the Christians' God was the one true God amongst the pantheon of deities she had encountered. She began to read the Bible.

"On the first night," she explained, "you opened your Bible and read, 'In the beginning God created the heaven and the earth.'[45] Something said to me, 'This is it... this is the God behind everything.' Every time I saw the sun or the moon, I prayed. Every time I saw an idol or a shrine, I prayed. But here... here, behind it all, was the living God."

On the final night her son came to the meeting. I remember seeing him on the back row, chain smoking, with his feet propped up on the bench in front. Grandma Hisasue, unable to get to church herself, sent him to learn more about her new faith. He started to bring his wife and daughter. One by one, through Grandma Hisasue's testimony, her family members became Christians and each in turn was baptized, until thirteen of them were regular members of the congregation.

In another town seven young apple farmers came forward at the end of the meetings. They faced little antagonism to their new faith until they decided they must be baptized. Their fathers were quick to express their opposition.

"If our sons become 'real' Christians," they argued,

"who will care for us when we die? They will abandon the reverence of their ancestors."

In the end, only one of the seven, an orphan, was baptized. Years later, when I visited the region, one of the fathers apologized to me.

"This year is the centenary of apple growing in Aomori. The government invited descendants of the missionaries who brought the first apple saplings from Pennsylvania to come here. Rich landowners were pocketing our ancestors' profits from rice growing. It was the missionaries who saw the plight of the farmers. The apple trees gave the farmers another source of income. I have learned that Christianity is a good religion."

His admiration of Christianity, regrettably, went no further than this.

One tent meeting seemed doomed from the start. We had inordinate problems securing a site large enough for our tent. The weather was atrocious. And, bizarrely, our Japanese evangelist chose to preach every night on the subject of death. There was a group of five high-school boys who attended. They always stayed on, asking questions, and weren't prepared to leave until we had answered them all. At the penultimate meeting we were disappointed to find them missing. As we packed things away, one of them raced into the tent with tragic news. His friend, a school *sumo* champion, had drowned in the river that evening.

"He had become a Christian," the boy told us. "He chose 'Jesus Christ' as his wrestling name. He wanted everyone to know he believed in Jesus."

This was not the first time I had seen a commitment closely followed by unexpected death. An assistant at a store in Goshogawara stayed behind after a tent meeting. He wanted to believe, and we talked late into the evening before we finally prayed with him. The following afternoon he was walking beneath an advertising arch that was being erected when the construction slipped from its moorings and fell on him. Many years before, in Berri, a couple of men, who lived in digs with me, had come to church and I had talked with them about finding salvation in Christ. Later in the week I was puzzled to find their room empty. The landlady told me that they had been killed in a motorcycle accident. Such experiences were a salutary lesson to me that we must use the opportunities we are given to tell others the gospel.

It was the prevalence of TV sets in the late fifties that killed much of the enthusiasm for our meetings. Increasing prosperity, in a land that had been bled dry by its own war effort and decimated by its opponents, was by no means a bad thing, but groups who had previously gathered in the arcades to view the latest game of baseball or cooking demonstrations, disappeared into insularity behind the walls of their homes to watch this newly acquired instant entertainment. Consumerism also slowly siphoned off our crowds. The male population, driven by exacting expectations in the workplace, became hard to reach. Many men would exhaust themselves with work, labouring morning, noon and night. A new generation, who knew nothing and were told nothing of the war, grew up. Shinto and Buddhism regained their prominence in the hierarchy of devotion. Our Sunday schools dwindled from fifty or a hundred down to a mere handful of children. Our evening meetings were reduced to a few faithful believers.

The post-war years had seemed full of promise. Christianity, it was said, would fill the "spiritual vacuum". In reality the Japanese, while politely fascinated by this "foreign" religion, stayed within the bounds of their traditions. In the late nineteenth century missionaries, allied with a rapid growth of the indigenous church, had also savoured the prospect of seeing Japan evangelized. The country would become Christian before the end of the century, they had predicted.[46] Yet Japan had closed ranks and the revival had petered out. For different reasons the extravagant aspirations of the 1950s were similarly deflated. Churches were planted but congregations remained small. Converts entered into faith but after a few years drifted out of the doors, drawn away by the exceptional pressures of daily life, by debt, by drink. Even today Japan has largely resisted any change in its religious make-up. Eighty-four per cent of its population are classed as Shinto or Buddhist, while a minute 0.7 per cent are Christian.

It was in perseverance with individuals that lasting fruit was borne. One of these was Ito-san, a plasterer, who lived in Goshogawara. Inspired by the story of Gideon, he tore down all the idols in his home. Berated by his mother for his rash behaviour, he was terrified of what his father would say. Nevertheless, he finished the job and put up a poster of Jesus washing his disciples' feet in the home shrine, telling his mother that out of the millions of gods in Japan, there wasn't one that would wash feet.

His father was both shocked and humiliated by his son's actions. "Son," he agonized, "if you become a Christian, I shall have to become half Christian and half Buddhist!"

Unable to get to church on Sunday due to the demands of his employers, Ito started his own business and built it up into the largest construction company in the city. Sundays were left free for his workforce to attend a service, and he dedicated the first tenth of all his income to God. When he was not able to find enough work for his men, he would often rise early and pray for new contracts, testifying how God, time after time, had met the need.

Ito was not easily dissuaded once he had put his mind to something. In early spring he asked to be baptized in the river, like Jesus. We stood amongst blocks of floating ice, the wind cutting through us, as I pushed him beneath the freezing water. I am sure he will never forget his baptism. Nor will I!

Two years later his mother made a commitment. His father had been warned that his "crazy" son would bring the punishment of the ancestors on the family, but, in time, he too became a Christian.

Over the first eighteen years of our marriage Evelyn and I rarely settled for long in one place. In 1959 we left Goshogawara and visited Australia and Britain. We then enjoyed two years in the wonderfully named Ajigasawa, one of the many neglected fishing towns on the Aomori coast; a place steeped in superstition. Laid out over three or so miles and nowhere deeper than four houses, its geography provided a constant challenge to maintaining a committed congregation. The church also suffered due to missionaries constantly being moved on. Ajigasawa had six workers come and go within four years.

"It's hardly worthwhile learning your names," one church member commented to the latest arrivals. "Missionaries change places so fast."

From Ajigasawa we moved to Hirosaki for another two-year stint, then had a year's deputation in the UK, and then were assigned to work in Otaru on the northern island of Hokkaido. We stayed there five years. Following another visit to the UK, we worked in Hachinohe City on the east coast of Honshu. Our home was a draughty, dilapidated dump on an unmade dirt road, with an open sewer running past the front door. Finally, in 1973, we arrived in Aomori City, where I had started my missionary career in earnest nineteen years before. This neat circle was broken by shattering news from OMF. Just a few months after settling back into ministry in Aomori, following another tour of the UK in 1975, we were informed we must return to Britain.

For much of my ministry I was often away from home, travelling from village to town to city, leading missions, preaching and teaching. Evelyn stayed at home caring for the boys and Liz. As each of the children grew old enough to start school, they went off to boarding-school – OMF's "Chefoo" in Japan – just as my sister and I had. Once they reached secondary school age, they moved to school in Britain and were only able to see us during the summer holidays. I was only too aware that my parents had made the same heartbreaking decisions I was now making, and I knew what the cost had been to me as a child.

It was this separation that brought us to one of the most challenging periods of our lives, for we found ourselves at odds with our UK colleagues. We must go back to Britain and take responsibility for our children, we were told. We must see them settled in the UK before being allowed to go back to the mission field. Once again we had to learn that our only sufficiency was in God. It was not going to be an easy lesson.

抑えた声

Osaetakoe
(Muffled Voices)

It is hard to recall how different the world of communication was before the Internet, broadband, email and cheap international phone calls existed. The 1970s saw tremendous changes in lifestyle, but letters still took a week to travel to the other side of the world, and rarely would one pick up the telephone and think to dial another country. Christians and Christian organizations were not immune from failing to communicate well.

On our 1975 visit to Britain we were presented with a dilemma we found difficult to resolve: a choice between leaving four children at boarding-school or setting aside our call to Japan. Danny, now seventeen, was at Monkton Combe School, Bath. Philip, John and Liz were attending King Edward's School, near Guildford. Friends and family opposed our return to Japan without our children. Unexpectedly, even colleagues in the UK cast doubts on the propriety of our plans. On the other hand, OMF missionaries in Japan and Japanese Christians were encouraging us to return to the mission field. My own "love/hate" relationship with the organization's boarding-school policies (which have now long since been superseded) only served to complicate the issues. In the end we decided that we must stay in the UK.

It was in these circumstances that Revd David Pawson's

sermon at Milmead Church in Guildford tore like a thunderbolt through our intentions.

"Jeremiah was in an unresponsive ministry for forty years," he preached, seemingly picking us out from the sea of faces in front of him. "If you have been called into God's ministry and are thinking of quitting… Don't! God is on your side." He quoted Romans chapter 11: "'For God's gifts and his call are irrevocable.'[47] He never withdraws them when once they are given, and he does not change his mind about those to whom he gives his grace or to whom he sends his call."

Evelyn and I wrestled with God over this. Paul was not addressing our missionary calling, but… it wasn't our calling, it was God who had called us.

The sudden reversal of our decision no doubt did little to enamour us to the OMF administration as we shuffled our way around revised arrangements, awkwardly and belatedly asking for help. It was, frankly, something of a relief to get back to Aomori and to be welcomed by the church there. Our Japanese friends, without our knowledge, had paid the deposit on a home for us. A rich property developer had offered to build a flat on his company parking lot, with a nice room in which to hold church services and teach English. The work began to prosper. It seemed as though the rewards of obedience were being reaped.

But we had been at the new Bible Centre less than two months when letters from Britain started to arrive. Confusing letters. Danny had left school before completing his "A" Levels. Danny was doing very well in his studies. Danny was not well. Danny was fine. Danny didn't want to come to Japan. Philip and John were failing in their work at school. We must come home to care for the four children. Our children were becoming estranged from us…

I had been on the mission field for twenty-three years when, in early 1976, we received the letter from OMF instructing us to return to the UK. One evening Evelyn and I took refuge in Hezekiah's approach to bad news, laying out before God the letter we had received telling us to return. I awoke just before dawn. Beside the bed was a figure, a distinct presence, though in the dark I could make out no features.

"Danny's all right." The words were clear; compelling words of reassurance.

It seemed I was on holy ground. I knew I was not imagining it. I woke Evelyn and told her we should take communion together. After prayer we both slept soundly, assured that God was with us. It was a unique experience.

What did become clear in the midst of all this ambiguity was that we were not being told the full story. In the end it seemed to come down to a pint of beer, worth about 32 pence then. But the price to OMF's sensibilities and the church in Aomori was substantially higher. Evelyn, James and I were flown back to Britain in February 1976. Danny met us at the airport. His enthusiastic welcome and that from Philip, John and Liz were sufficient to reassure us that we were in no way losing the love of our family.

Our friends in Japan were bewildered at our sudden departure. We had returned to them in obedience to God. Now we were being pulled away again. God was at work; why would we leave them? We seemed to be at the heart of a spiritual battle. The crux of the matter was that Danny had stepped off the "narrow path" and in the company of an older friend had been down to the pub for a pint. The hostel parents where he was staying were not impressed. Channels of communication had become choked, gateways to a solution were blocked for the want of clarity. It was like echoes caught in a cavern. Somehow the repercussions had reverberated, picking up negative vibrations from other sources, and the issue was amplified way beyond its true seriousness.

Whatever the rights and wrongs for those of us who were involved, it was a painful time. With no immediate prospect of returning to Japan, we had to resign our membership of OMF. After a lifetime of association with the organization, this hurt deeply. As a consequence, we were suddenly without their pastoral and monetary support. At the start of the next financial quarter OMF kindly sent us our remittance. They were not comfortable with leaving a family of five children without funds. I returned the cheque with a carefully worded letter. We appreciated the kindness but the mission was no longer responsible for us. We had to rely on God to provide.

I had first truly appreciated God's ability to supply all my needs through walking five miles in the pouring rain, frustrated with him for not supplying the bus fare I needed. I was a student at Melbourne Bible College and was leading a midweek evening meeting at the church I had been assigned to. I only had enough cash for the train fare to get within a bus ride of the church. I had prayed for God to provide the bus fare. The extra money had not appeared. As I watched my bus leave the station without me for the want of a few pennies, I was not terribly happy. My mood blackened with the gathering clouds. I settled into a long-winded gripe against God as the first drops of rain signalled the fact that I was going to get very wet. I prayed. I sang spiritual songs. The rain continued falling and my irritation grew. The young people roared in laughter as I made my bedraggled entrance just in time for the service. I adopted a spirit of stoicism and did my job. It was still raining when I contemplated the five-mile walk back to the station.

"Want a lift?" asked Roy, one of the church members. He owned an egg-delivery business and had his truck waiting.

"Sure do," I replied.

"Steve!" There was someone chasing after me as I gratefully hauled myself into the cab. He drew level and thrust an envelope at me.

"Steve, my dad told me to give you this." His father was a baggage porter down at the docks.

"Er… thanks." It was clear this was money. I was beginning to regret my earlier strop with God. But God hadn't done with me yet. As we reached the station, Roy pushed his hand into his jacket pocket.

"Here, let me pay your train fare."

I protested.

"I've a bit extra tonight. I'd like to pay."

"No," I persisted, "I've got to go out to the airport to meet my sister, Ruth."

"Then I'll pay her fare as well," he laughed and pushed money into my hand.

Later I opened the envelope I had received. There was 40 Australian pounds in it – a considerable sum to me.

Remarkably, the porter who gave me this money met my needs again around seven years later. This time I was in Australia with Evelyn and Danny. We had taken a taxi to the docks to board a ship for Europe. As the taxi pulled up a man opened the door.

"I've been waiting for you. I'll take your bags."

I was embarrassed. "I can't tip him," I whispered to Evelyn. "We haven't enough money."

But there was no use protesting – he was already leading the way. We could only straggle along behind, rueing the anticipated cost of his unasked-for services.

"There you go." He showed us into our cabin.

As gracefully as I could, I put my hand in my pocket.

"Oh, no…" He reached out and held my arm. "I've sons at the church you were at in Dingley." He drew a crumpled tangle of notes from his own pocket. "I promised God I'd give you all the tips I got today."

His generosity amounted to 44 Australian pounds – more than enough to cover our expenses on the voyage.

While in Ireland on that same tour, I was again humbled by the willingness of the most ordinary folk to obey God's command to give. At one meeting I was approached by a farmer.

"Mr Metcalf, I've a gift for you." He handed me a sizeable packet. "I've been waiting three years for someone from the OMF to stop by. I told God I'd give every ten-shilling note I got to the OMF." There were over 700 ten-shilling notes in the parcel – £368 in total.

His faithfulness was in direct contrast to the church treasurer I had encountered in Berri (another farmer). Irritated, no doubt, at the audacity of a posh-accented jackaroo barely out of his teens preaching to the church committee on the principles of tithing, he took me to task.

"It's all right for Steve, on his salary, to talk about tithing." By this he meant that 10 per cent of not a lot was a small sum to find each week for the collection plate. "But it's ridiculous. If I tithed, I would be paying for the whole church budget myself."

Given we were discussing the financial straits the church was in, there was an amusing absurdity in his objections.

Some years later Evelyn and I were facing another financial crisis. The pound had dropped from 1,000 yen to the pound to just 400. Gifts from the UK were worth less than half of their previous value. We had school fees to find for the children. The mission would pay 70 per cent, but we must find the additional 30 per cent. The crisis was compounded when the funds for the 70 per cent failed to appear. It was five months before the money was sent to us. In the meanwhile, however, the yen had weakened and the mission's "70 per cent" now matched the full amount of the fees.

Arriving in Britain in 1976, and no longer members of OMF, we became very dependent on the generosity of others. A temporary home was found for us in Four Marks, close to King Edward's School. A friend supplied us with a car. Someone left a huge food hamper on our doorstep. The local church gave prayer and practical support. We felt powerless to provide for ourselves. It was stressful occupying someone else's home with five active children around the house. Hard cash was an issue. I needed to find a job. Inflation was high, heading for 23 per cent; unemployment stood at 6 per cent. I trailed down to the Job Centre to be told I was too well qualified. Yet we could only be amazed as God continued to provide for us from the unlikeliest of places. Unexpectedly we received financial gifts from Canada and Cambodia. Another cheque arrived from Japan. In all the years we had been on the mission field, we had never received such large amounts of money.

It took a job advert cutting in the *Times*, sent to us from Exeter, to help us feel that long-term relief was on its way.

St Helen's Bishopsgate in London needed a Christian worker, fluent in Japanese, to minister to Japanese businessmen in the city. There could be few qualified for such a post that particular year, and I quickly secured an interview. I had no doubt this was God's provision. Revd Dick Lucas invited me into his office, said a prayer and then began asking me questions. Finally he closed in prayer.

"Mr Metcalf," he said carefully, "you're not the person we are looking for. God must have someone else in mind. Your place is in Japan, not here."

Excusing himself, he went out to speak to his secretary. I felt another thunderbolt rip through our plans. Surely this had to be the way forward. What did he mean, my place was "in Japan"? The door was shut. S-H-U-T. And we had our fingers caught in the jamb. As I left, Dick handed me a cheque for £300 – a more than generous gift from St Helen's. All the way back to Four Marks on the train I took God to task over the situation. I felt like a lame man. I had a deep desire to walk on my own legs but was being carried along by events and the kindness of others. All God seemed to be saying was, "Wait… until you find out what happens."

和解

Wakai
(Reconciliation)

I never did find a job.

Evelyn was as confused as I was over the situation. Like me, she had pinned our hopes on the position at St Helen's. The children were guaranteed schooling until the summer, but we had no idea what would happen beyond that. We contemplated moving to Northern Ireland, closer to Evelyn's home.

The rejection we felt allowed us to come to the place God had prepared for us. We reconciled ourselves to waiting for the situation to be resolved. God's provision, like the widow of Zarephath's jar of flour and cruse of oil, never failed. When the owner of the house in Four Marks returned from his visit to the USA, we were offered the use of a thatched cottage close by in the trim village of Upper Wield, a few miles north. It was a long hot summer, the longest dry spell on record, but when the rains finally came we found the local fields covered in large-headed edible mushrooms. In the early autumn I carried home baskets of blackberries for Evelyn to boil into jam and bake into pies.

Unused to being "idle", I became disheartened. I felt discarded by OMF, sidelined by God. We were not invited to share our excitement at the development of the work in Aomori. The normal round of deputation talks was denied us. Nobody – neither the mission nor ministers – seemed interested in our stories of Japan. Finally, our pastor asked me to preach at the church in his stead. Paradoxically, given the circumstances, I was led to speak on Paul's admonition to Timothy – "Stir up the gift of God, which is in thee."[48] I experienced a great liberty in preaching. The congregation were attentive, responsive even, but as they filed out nobody mentioned the sermon. I was relieved to notice one woman hanging back. Here would be some solace to my self-doubt!

"Thank you," she enthused as she left. "The last hymn we sang was one of my favourites…"

My deflation was complete!

Some weeks later the church minister stopped by. "You really addressed in a positive way an issue the church has been struggling with," he told me. "A good number of people have commented on your sermon. Some even thought I must have briefed you on the situation."

It was a very small thing, but I hung onto it in the months ahead. God could still use me, even if the rest of my world appeared to have abandoned me.

Our road back to Japan began with the intervention of the General Director of OMF, Michael Griffiths. He and his wife, Valerie, had served in Japan, before moving to the OMF international headquarters in Singapore. His children were at the same school as Philip, John and Liz. We chatted at an open day. I was blunt in my estimation of the situation. Why had no one talked to us or to our children before hauling us back to the UK?

Slowly the tangled threads of miscommunication were unravelled, knots of personal prejudice unpicked, lines of responsibility realigned. People began to question and then change the rules that forced veteran missionaries out of fruitful fields of ministry. International counsel decided that we must be the final arbitrators of our future. In reality, we were apparently left with little choice. The UK hostel we had formerly used was closed to our children. Without suitable accommodation for them, there was no way for us to leave for Asia. We wrote to OMF and indicated we would have to remain in Britain.

Once more Michael Griffiths rallied the mission's resources; another hostel in the UK was found for the children and our membership of OMF reinstated. In November 1976, just eight months after leaving, we arrived back at the Bible Centre in Aomori. Danny had a place at Art College in London. Philip and John, close to major examinations, remained at King Edward's School. Liz, now thirteen, chose to return with Evelyn, James and I to Japan to complete her schooling there.

We often questioned why these events had disrupted our ministry. Whilst in Japan we had felt that any advance for the kingdom of God was only won through a battle with spiritual darkness. Surrounded by the very pleasant, green pastures of rural England, we had experienced the same encounter – warfare conducted in prayer, in which the victory was the prising open of a door to ongoing missionary service.

In our absence, the work in Aomori City had been taken on by a couple from New Zealand, who had been pulled from their language studies to fill the gap. We persevered with the small Sunday congregation and outreach to ones and twos, but after eighteen months we again moved. Sendai, on the east coast of Honshu, was a thriving metropolis, with a population approaching a million – it was very different to the rural ambience of Aomori. Bisected by the Hirose River, this "City of Trees" was famous for its greenery; the main thoroughfares were lined with slender, vase-like zelkova trees. In the past the residents had been encouraged to plant trees and transform their home environs into *yashikirin*, household forests used to furnish their families with wood. Sadly, much of this ecological wealth had been destroyed by the bombs of World War II, and the city had never fully recovered the riches of its traditional reputation.

The Sendai church was close to the river in the city centre and comprised seven baptized men and eight women. Whilst this OMF initiative had grown rapidly, we discovered that few of the locals were really interested in Christianity. Hardly any of the city's churches had more than forty members. The region boasted three large Christian colleges, but the majority of students and staff were Buddhists. We suffered from the "in group/out group" mentality of the Japanese. Belonging to an "in group", such as a company or school, allowed colleagues to disclose information. People outside this unit had no rights to knowledge shared within the group. The situation was exacerbated by the concept of *wa*, harmony, combined with a veneer of courtesy laid over any matter which may create conflict. For the Japanese it was esteemed wiser to tell lies than to disturb the delicate *wa* of cross-cultural sensitivities. As foreigners, we were definitely in the "out group" and more easily placated with false optimistic noises of interest than outright rejection.

Despite the general ambivalence, our church did grow. A year later numbers had swelled to over twenty regular members, people coming from all four corners of the city into our inadequate church premises. They were a diverse lot. A high-school student brought Koizumi to us. This young man had left his university application papers on a train.

"You'll never get those back," the station master had told him as Koizumi had pleaded for help.

Koizumi was desperate. He prayed, "Oh, God, I don't know if you exist, but… if you help me find these forms, I'll worship you."

To his astonishment, a man turned up at his door with the papers. Anxious to discover which god had answered his prayers, the young man told a Christian in his building the story.

"You need to go to our church," the boy told him, and so Koizumi joined our fellowship.

It was unusual for an older person to come to us alone. More often than not we attracted such folk through the witness of younger family members. One day, a widower of seventy-eight wandered into church. Lost in loneliness, he had decided that he must re-educate himself if he was to cope in old age. As a journalist he had travelled overseas and visited the huge cathedrals of Christian countries, where he had sensed awe, the presence of God. He understood little of the gospel, but was impressed that every Christian must make a personal commitment to Christ.

Mukade-san was a locksmith, who sported a sizeable tattoo on his back and shoulders. He worked day and night to develop a business in stained glass. Caught in a regime of overwork to sustain his business, Mukade, a keen believer, stopped attending church. His wife continued to come, but eventually the need to care for two children kept her away, and we lost contact. One Sunday morning Mrs Mukade reappeared with her children in tow. Her second baby had a foot turned in and the doctor had declared that she would have to live with the deformity for the rest of her life. Mrs Mukade had begun to pray day and night for healing. She felt that she was too great a sinner for God to answer her prayer, but one morning she had wakened to find that the baby's foot was normal. Now, she had returned to share this miracle with us.

Takahashi-san was a translator who contacted me over the content of a book he was working on, the biography of Herbert Taylor, a Christian American industrialist.[49] Convinced of the rightness of Marxism, Takahashi was completely ignorant of Christianity. He had no idea what "born again" might mean, so he was unable to translate it into his native language. Although he was initially reluctant to include "a lot of nonsense and religious jargon", the powerful testimony of Taylor challenged him and he began to study the Scriptures.

Then, there was the fast-food shop owner, Endo-san, whose wife's sister had become a Christian, but who showed little interest in the Bible studies we conducted in his home. One evening the poor man was on the point of exhaustion when I greeted him in his hallway.

"Ogenki desu ka?" ("How are you?") I asked politely.

"I haven't slept in days," he replied wearily.

"Why?"

"A thief has been raiding our shop. Broken the locks. Stolen our takings. I've waited up several nights for him." He shrugged, "It's no use."

I suggested we pray. He looked at me sceptically.

"Our God answers prayer," I insisted. "Come and sit down. We'll all pray for you and your thief."

The next day his wife phoned me.

"He caught the thief! Endo caught the thief. Locked him

in the shop, took his photograph and called the police!"

Impressed by this God who answered prayers, Endo announced he wanted to become a Christian. As a result we were able to open up new work in another area of the city and plant another growing church.

These new believers encouraged us, but in truth our "successes" remained small in the face of a population to whom Christianity remained an alien religion. In 1982 I recorded in a letter home that Christians represented just 0.2 per cent of Japan's 119 million people.[50] Someone wryly noted that on Christmas Eve Japan became fashionably Christian, but by New Year the Shinto shrines and Buddhist temples were back in vogue. The election in 1978 of Ohira Masayoshi, the nation's second Christian Prime Minister, raised our hopes, but his decision to take part in ancestral worship at national shrines – a political prayer for popularity – proved a disappointment. The nationwide depth of interest in Christianity shown by the post-war generation of the 1950s has never yet been recaptured.

The film *Chariots of Fire*, released in 1981, renewed awareness of Eric Liddell and his Christian faith. Initially the Japanese reviewers were sceptical, decrying it as a ridiculous film depicting the rivalry between Jews and Christians or declaring patronizingly that the nation would not understand it. Perhaps there was official embarrassment that Liddell had died in a Japanese POW camp, though that information is only allocated one line of subtitles as the film comes to its conclusion. Shown at first only in minor theatres in Japan, the film's popularity gathered momentum and it is still a film people want to see. It also brought the local media to our doorstep requesting interviews, a scenario that still occurs twenty-eight years later as TV companies, journalists and biographers, anxious to meet the man who received Liddell's running shoes, come looking for a story!

In 1985 we returned from another visit to the UK for our seventh and final term of service. Retirement was on the horizon. We did not go back to Sendai. This time Evelyn and I found ourselves scanning columns of government statistics and poring over maps of Tokyo in search of a home for a new initiative in the capital itself. Thirty years earlier Tokyo had been better served by the national church community and OMF's emphasis had been on the neglected areas of north Honshu and Hokkaido where churches were few and far between. In the 1960s, as industrialization shrank the rural workforce, the migration of workers into expanding cities had decimated farming towns and villages. Tokyo had seen massive growth, with satellite cities of one or two hundred thousand people sprouting up wherever skyscrapers could be constructed. There was a huge need to establish churches to impact these new communities, but local believers lacked the finances to secure land for building.

Evelyn and I drove miles in a borrowed car, rode trains and buses from one cityscape to the next, surveying property and prospects – a distinct contrast to my meanderings through the fishing villages of Aomori Prefecture in 1954. Overnight, houses were being completed and new owners moved in. Blocks of fourteen or fifteen storeys were being built, and they would be filled with 150 families within a week. Mortgages were high, interest rates formidable, but there was no shortage of new buyers. Our search finally brought us to Urayasu. This former fishing village lay to the east of Tokyo city centre on the far side of the Edo River. Expansion had

177

been achieved by pushing thousands of tons of landfill into Tokyo Bay, creating a flat expanse of tarmac and concrete in an "American" regular lattice of streets. Declared a city in April 1981, the area's popularity soared a couple of years later with the opening of Disneyland. By the time we settled on one of its many estates, an area accommodating 900 families, the population of Urayasu had reached 100,000.

We started with nothing in the way of church members. There was just Evelyn, myself, our prayers and God. Having God alongside was good! Slowly people began to respond. Two years after we arrived, I remember sitting in Granny Takada's garden, waiting for the July spectacle of Urayasu's annual *hanabi* festival of fireworks to erupt into the skies above us. Granny Takada had been a Christian for many years and moved into a home close to us. Amongst the watchers was Usui-san, a civil servant with the water board, who had found himself in conflict with office colleagues because they insisted on booking work hours while they played *mah-jong* and drank *sake* into the evening. His wife, a Christian, had encouraged him to anchor his ethics in God's ways, not just his own sense of honour. Now he had made a commitment.

Toda-san was another Urayasu church member. He had worked for an airline that had collapsed with the instability in Lebanon in the early eighties. I was introduced to him by an American called Pete, a disturbed, uncouth individual who suffered with schizophrenia. Pete, having fled harsh medical treatment in the USA, had travelled the world and was a fantastic linguist. Somehow Toda, a thin, middle-aged bachelor of around forty-five, had become Pete's carer.

"Who are you and why have you come here?" Toda asked me.

"I am a Christian missionary."

"I read the English papers. I see lots of quotes from the Bible. Your religion interests me but I have never found time to study it. You are a teacher?"

"Yes."

"Then you will teach me."

Toda's appetite for Bible study was immense. He was always urging me to go on when I looked like stopping. One New Year's morning I called on him. He was practising his calligraphy skills. With fast, fluid strokes of his brush down the paper he painted the words, "God said, 'Let there be light': and there was light."[51] That was a significant moment for him; through his artwork God's word had indeed brought divine illumination into his life.

He put up a plain wooden cross in the porch of his home, a sign of his commitment to Christ. At Easter 1988, when we had our first baptism service, Toda, who had been with us from the beginning, was one of those we baptized. Later he became a lay pastor within the church and helped us secure a contract on a coffee shop that had been bankrupted. It was an ideal setting to attract new members. Toda and I found wood to make three crosses down at the local timber yard.

"It was Simon who carried Jesus' cross, wasn't it?" asked Toda.

"Yes."

"I would have liked to have done that…"

Toda continued to care for Pete until Pete's medication finally took his life. Toda's home, Pete always said, was a place of refuge from the evil that haunted him.

We said our farewells to Urayasu in August 1990. On our last Sunday we baptized twelve of the congregation.

We left behind eighteen baptized believers and had around thirty regular attendees at our services. These are not statistics that seem worthy of mention where only success in ministry is deemed newsworthy. But Japan is not a success story for Christian mission. It is a place that requires dedication to the few who follow and unflagging perseverance amongst the many who do not. There is much joy in heaven over any individual who trusts in Christ, and so it is in Japan.

Evelyn was sixty-six, I was approaching sixty-three. Between us we had over seventy years on the mission field. Our Japanese friends were reluctant to see us leave. "But now is a good time for you," they argued. "You have all this experience."

Old age was deemed an advantage! And perhaps they were right, because as we moved into retirement the following year, I was invited to be involved in ministry at the Japanese Christian Fellowship in London, a role I fulfilled for another fifteen years.

平成
Heisei
(Peace Everywhere)

On 7 January 1989 in an august room of the Imperial Palace in Tokyo, the stiff mantle of heaven's sovereignty slipped from the shoulders of Michinomiya Hirohito and was picked up by his son, Akihito. The late Emperor – *Tenno*,[52] as his subjects named him – was eighty-seven years old. It was revealed that, for over three months, he had been suffering with duodenal cancer. In a legacy stretching back to 660 BC, he was the one hundred and twenty-fourth incumbent of the Chrysanthemum Throne in a nominally unbroken succession of rulers, some of them token leaders, others exercising god-like authority. He held the extraordinary distinction of being the first Emperor in centuries to be the son of his predecessor's official wife. In 1921, as crown prince, he had been the first of his echelon to visit Europe, touring six nations. His death brought to an end a longer-serving reign than any of his ancestors – sixty-two turbulent years. Within that time – the ill-named *Showa* (the Era of Enlightened Peace) – he had witnessed Japan rise to rule East Asia and fall into desolation. He had seen the demeaning destruction of his nation and watched her ascend again on a wave of industrial and economic prowess to the heights of world domination occupied by her conquerors.

Tenno was an enigmatic figure to his subjects. Before and during Japan's assault on Asia in the 1930s and 1940s he remained obscured beneath a cloak of divinity; a delicate, indistinct status derived from a lineage originating with Amaterasu, the Sun Goddess, in a land where the divide between deity and humanity is at best vague and finds no comparison in a Western understanding of omnipotence, omniscience and omnipresence. His coronation in November 1928 was a sumptuous spectacle of Shinto pageantry, the 400-mile route from Tokyo to Kyoto sanded, raked and prayed over by thousands of worshippers. His enthronement, where he informed Amaterasu that he was assuming the throne of his ancestors and declared, like his ancestors, that the people were now his children, was hallowed by an omen of good fortune – a rainbow, appearing above the hills in the northern skies. In 1940, the 2,600th anniversary of the founding of the empire further strengthened the already strong links between Shinto and State. Each morning at 6 a.m. city households were wakened with the blast of a bugle call broadcast into their homes, a signal for them to bow low towards the Palace prior to receiving lengthy instruction from the government on how to conduct themselves. The population were groomed to a belief in Japan's ultimate victory, the certainty of her natural supremacy and the rightness of her endeavour to release Asia from colonial oppression; views reinforced by the occasional iconic appearances of their Emperor in military uniform.

When, on 15 August 1945, Hirohito, the unassailable "voice of the crane",[53] pronounced on the radio in the arcane speech of the imperial court that Japan would accept the terms of the Allies' treaty, it was the first time the people had heard their Emperor speak publicly. Wrapped in shadows, the message created confusion, until an official clarification that the war had ended was issued. After defeat Hirohito made a public declaration renouncing divinity, further confounding the principles the nation had been nurtured on.[54] From then on he embodied a commendable image of his people, a diminutive, passive man speaking of peace. He had a love of Japanese haiku poetry, was a recognized expert in marine biology and, eccentrically, wore a Mickey Mouse watch he acquired on a visit to the USA. Two decades on from his death, his culpability in the war remains a mystery, polarized protagonists in the debate portraying him as racist hawk or frustrated dove.

Emperor Akihito replaced Hirohito with his own *Heisei* ("Peace Everywhere") Era. The quiet self-restraint of cancelled festivals and parties that had settled over the country as Tenno battled with cancer gave way to a widespread willingness to talk about the war. Relieved of a duty of respect for the deceased Emperor, people began to ask questions about Japan's role in the conflict. Documentaries appeared on TV. Soldiers published their memoirs. Allegiance to imperial orders had meant that "duty [was] weightier than a mountain while death [was] lighter than a feather"[55]. POWs, who endured the unspeakable ignominy of being captured by the Allied forces, lived with the deep disgrace this brought to themselves and their family honour. Many had lived under false names in internment camps; some had not returned to their homes on release. "My life was as good as ended when the Americans plucked me from the water", wrote one sailor of his rescue from the sea off the coast of Indonesia. "I could no longer live in Japanese society."[56] For forty years it was as though the nation had held its breath, colluded in a pact of ignorance, unwilling or unable to address the shame of defeat. After the death of Hirohito the change in attitude was evident. I found Japanese Christians, knowing my personal circumstances, were suddenly eager for my opinions of the war. In fact, people from all walks of life seemed interested. Any conversation on the subject drew in bystanders. The war had been fought for the Emperor, they said. Capitulation had been an unthinkable loss of face for him and the nation.

In Japan the dead are always with you. The honour of the departed is as important as that of the living. At the heart of Tokyo, adjacent to the Imperial Palace, is the Yasukuni Shrine, established by Hirohito's grandfather in 1869. In a poem the Meiji Emperor[57] assured soldiers that "those of you who fought and died for your country… your names will live forever at this shrine". It is a place of worship, not just remembrance, enshrining the spirits of the dead, elevating them to "divinities". Such is the innate depth of spiritual sentiment that fourteen convicted Japanese war criminals were secretly enshrined at the site in 1978, a controversial act that Hirohito opposed and one which brought bitter condemnation from other Asian nations.

With the birth of new generations of Japanese children, the pact of ignorance has been coupled with indifference. Starved of information about the war at school, where textbooks are silent on the historical reality of Japan's crimes against humanity, her youth believe that what happened was so long ago that it has ceased to matter. When I talked of the consequences of the war, I heard comments like "a complete waste of time", "outdated" and "too far in the past".

I met a schoolteacher at the Japanese Embassy in London who had taken graduating high-school students to Beijing to meet their Chinese counterparts. Questions in open forum about the war in China showed the ignorance of the Japanese; in fact, some declared that they didn't even know Japan had fought with China. Pressed for help, the teacher, ignorant himself, had to bluff his way out of the dilemma, stating that the war had been an unhappy affair and was not part of their curriculum. Tempers flared when the Japanese students were asked about the conflicts in Korea and Vietnam. How could they know so much about these wars and yet so little about their own history?

For European nations the Pacific War is remote. Japan did not threaten the streets of London or Paris. Initially there was anger and odium over the inhuman prisons of East Asia, and in the years following the war few had a good word for the "Japs". Abhorrence, which was still alive in the seventies and eighties, has given way to ambivalence. In Asia it is different. Japan's apparent apathy to her history is a continuing affront to other nations where the past is not forgotten. China, a nation that has not yet buried the injustice of the Opium Wars of 1842 and 1860, has certainly not forgotten the horrible wounds she suffered under the Japanese a century later. The "Rape of Nanjing" still runs like a bloody scar across relationships with her neighbour. The "triviality" of a controversial defeat of the national football team in Beijing by the Japanese team at the Asia Cup in 2004 sparked riots, the Japanese press naively asking why the Chinese should react so strongly.

In Korea, the demonstrations by women forced into prostitution for the "comfort" of Japanese soldiers are still waved away by Japanese politicians. Both South Korea and China have baulked at the Japanese Ministry of Education's recent approval of textbooks which distort death tolls, play down the sufferings of their nationals and deny "sex slaves" the dignity of a mention. Occasional apologies are undermined by official visits to the Yasukuni Shrine to honour the dead or statements serving internal political interests, rather than addressing the deeply felt emotions of neighbouring nations. Over and again I have explained to Japanese friends that reconciliation is dependent on understanding the grief of those whose families had suffered rape, torture, experiences of horrific death, loss of loved ones. An alliance of ignorance and indifference will never bring the forgiveness that is needed.

Some Japanese, however, have embraced the reality of the past and are reaching out to others, seeking true peace. In 1991, soon after our return to the UK, we were privileged to meet one of them.

組み合わせ

Kumiawase
(Dovetail)

The Kii Peninsula, Honshu Island's most southerly land-mass, lies around 250 miles south-west of Tokyo, protruding like a large thumb into the Pacific Ocean. It is a relatively remote area of immense natural beauty, sparingly populated due to the density of its forests of towering cedar, cypress and pine and the natural ruggedness of its mountainous topography. Beneath these evergreen canopies are secreted white-flowered spikes of japonica and large colonies of deinanthe, the tiniest of hostas and delicate wild orchids clinging to tree-bark. Lengthy river courses are persuaded through a labyrinth of interconnected valleys, press through the narrowest of gorges and plunge refreshingly over dramatic waterfalls.

Towards the distant southern tip of this peninsula, within the mountains, lies the village of Iruka.[58] To the west flows the imposing Kitayama River, famous for its precipitous cliffs and twisting ravines. To the east of Iruka are the *Senmaida*, a breath-taking staircase of over a thousand paddy fields, some of which, reputedly, could be hidden beneath a straw hat. On 18 June 1944, 300 British prisoners of war trudged into the village and were interned in the Osaka POW Number 16 Branch Camp.[59] Their arrival was part of a government plan to bolster the efforts of its indigenous workforce.[60] The prisoners were in the "employ" of the Ishihara Industry Company and made to work the local copper mines alongside Japanese miners and students. These were shadows of men – "physical wrecks", as one of them described their condition, weighing as little as seventy-four pounds. But in many respects they were the fortunate ones. They had been transferred from the nightmarish conditions of the camps constructing the Thai–Burma railway. These were infernal jails, where they had endured tropical heat, humidity and monsoon, had been afflicted with disease and deprivation, where they had been scarred by the acid cruelty of their captors. They had watched comrades die; but they had lived. Now they had outlasted the dangers of the notorious Japanese death-ships, which transported humans like cargo and ran the gauntlet of Allied aggression, and on which around 11,000 POWs lost their lives en route to Japan.

Each day the group were marched from their camp through the pine trees to a fork in the road. The path to the left would have taken them down the valley to the river and a route home, to freedom. Theirs was always the path to the right in the direction of the mines. More than half of them toiled in the pits, while the rest laboured in the ore-processing plant. They were provided with dry shelter and rough clothing and for the first few months the food was more plentiful and varied than their previous diet. But as the autumn descended into winter, food shortages began to bite and conditions deteriorated. Two members of the group succumbed early to heart failure due to beriberi and another to malaria. Over the next four months another six died of beriberi, two of pneumonia and one of pyaemia. Three suffered fatal head injuries and the last of the sixteen who died at Iruka had a heart attack.

Three weeks after the end of the war the POWs were

released. The surviving soldiers commemorated their comrades with the construction of a simple grave, a wooden cross and a plaque listing the names of those who had died. Open lorries collected the men from the camp and drove them down through the village before they finally took the left-hand fork in the road to freedom. I doubt if any of the 284 who made the journey back to Britain had the remotest intention of returning.

Keiko Nishi was born in Nishiyama, ten miles from Iruka, four years after the POWs left. As a child she could never have foreseen the significance that the strange unpretentious cross, surrounded by Buddhist graves in the local cemetery, would have for her. While studying in Tokyo, she fell in love with Paul Holmes, a Christian teacher at the university, and became a Christian herself. They married and, ten years later, came to live in London. In 1984 Paul was tragically killed in an air accident while on business in Bangladesh, and Keiko's world turned dark.

Returning to her home town four years later, Keiko visited the graveyard. The burial-place for the British POWs had been transformed. The site had always been maintained by a local senior citizens' group; their innate concern for the dead extended in traditional courtesy to the spirits whose relatives could not visit the cemetery. In 1987 a larger memorial had been constructed, with a marble plinth and a copper cross flanked by stone memorial plaques, one listing the soldiers' names, the other narrating a brief history. Keiko returned to Britain determined to tell ex-POWs at Iruka about the new memorial. In doing so she found fresh purpose for her life.

God had given her no easy commission. At the annual conference of the Far East Prisoners of War Association in

London in 1991, she encountered the enormity of her task. She was warned not to attend – a lone Japanese woman intruding on the private grief of more than a thousand veterans and their family members. As she held up pictures of Iruka, backs were turned. Insults were tossed like grenades in her direction. But from this uncertain start contacts were made and, in October 1992, nineteen of the "Iruka Boys", as Keiko called them, joined a congregation of local people in a Christian Service of Remembrance before the Iruka memorial. In that shared act of worship there was healing that uprooted the loathing which had lain buried for forty-seven hate-filled years.

Through our work with the Japanese Christian Fellowship in London, Evelyn and I were introduced to Keiko and asked to lead Bible studies for Japanese women at her home. Her reconciliation work between POWs and the Japanese was growing. She had formed an organization, now called Agape.[61] For a number of years Keiko encouraged me to join one of her tours, but it was 2003 before we were free to join twenty-two others headed for Japan. It was a decision which opened doors to ministry I had not anticipated; this book being the latest of them.

En route to Kyoto, the starting-point for our tour, I listened to the stories of my companions. Sir Sam Falle, before being rescued by the Japanese navy, had floated in the sea for around twenty-four hours after his destroyer, *HMS Encounter*, was sunk.

"We were off Indonesia in February '42. On the twenty-seventh we engaged a convoy fleet in the Java Sea. Things didn't go well for us. We were outnumbered and outgunned. All in all, we lost three cruisers and five destroyers against some serious damage to one of their destroyers.

"We survived the initial onslaught. Two days later we were caught in open water by four destroyers and six cruisers. We and an American destroyer were escorting the *Exeter* out of the battle zone. The *Exeter* went down and we lost sight of the Americans.

"Then we were hit. We were sitting motionless with forty-six guns trained on us. The captain gave the order to abandon ship. I jumped into the Java Sea and grabbed onto a float. One of the destroyers came close. I thought that was the end of it, but it sailed away, leaving us to our fates. I was in the water overnight.

"Then another Japanese destroyer, the *Ikazuchi*, turned up. They hauled us out of the sea. Gave us fresh clothes. Fed us. Eventually there were 300 of us on board! The captain told us, 'You have fought bravely. Now you are honoured guests of the Imperial Japanese Navy… Your government is very foolish to make war on Japan.' After that I was in POW camp.

"I've been in touch with one of the men who dragged me to safety. He got hold of an article I wrote about my experiences. He's visited me, now I'm meeting him in Japan."

We met Sir Sam's rescuer at Tokyo airport. Ex-gunnery officer Shunzo Tagami was a dapper little man with greying hair and the nicest of smiles. He told me he was a Christian and had been converted by some of his navy officers, who had studied English with missionaries before the war.

Jan Ruff-O'Herne, a Dutch woman, had been in the squalid, vermin-infested barracks of Ambarawa women's prison camp in Indonesia for the worst part of two years with her mother and two young sisters. On a hot humid Friday at the end of February 1944 single females aged seventeen and

191

over had been lined up and inspected by Japanese officers. Jan and fifteen other Dutch young women were driven away on the back of an open truck. Seven of them were deposited at a large colonial-style house, renamed by the Japanese as the "House of the Seven Seas". Jan was given her own bedroom, complete with a double bed. The girls' photographs were pinned to a board for Japanese soldiers to peruse in advance of making their selection.

"The house was a brothel. We were there to provide sexual pleasure for the military. I was twenty-one."

On the "opening night" Jan was raped by a fat, bald-headed Japanese. Over the course of the next three months she and the other girls were forced to have sex with at least ten Japanese men each night. If they tried to hide, they were beaten. Jan's only relief from this sordid nightmare was when a kindly Japanese acquaintance of her older sister paid to keep others from abusing her for two weeks.

"They took away my youth and my dignity. After the war I informed the British Army police, but nothing was done. I told my mother once but we never spoke of it again. It took me years to find the courage to speak out. I lived in silence with the horrific shame, the dirtiness, of it all.

"In 1992 some Korean women spoke up. I watched them on TV. They were sobbing for justice. They gave me courage. I wanted to hug them. I thought, now is my time."

Jan had written a book about her experiences[62] and had been a prominent spokeswoman at the International Public Hearing in Tokyo in December 1992 on the injustices suffered by women abused by Japanese soldiers.

"The men came back from the war with medals on their chests," she told me. "All these women came back with were scars."

Later Jan spoke at a Sunday service in a Japanese church. "I never lost my faith," she explained. "I used to pray day and night, 'Father, forgive them, for they do not know what they are doing.'"[63]

A Japanese lady rose from her seat. "My father was tried for war crimes. He was hung. I was never told what crime he had committed. There has been silence in Japan."

At the end of the service I watched Jan and this woman embrace. It was a deeply moving moment.

As part of our tour we visited a primary school where we all sat in groups with the children and answered their questions about what it was like to be a prisoner of war. When we finished I was approached by a middle-aged teacher and a journalist.

"We have learned a lot of new things today," they said. "The children are able to ask many questions we would never have the face to ask you."

We also visited Hiroshima and stood in the Peace Memorial Park in front of the arched cenotaph. Our conversation centred on whether the USA should have dropped the atom bomb within sight of Tokyo, away from civilian areas, as a warning of what was to come if the nation did not capitulate. We had gathered to honour the dead; those whose lives had been sacrificed so that we could obtain freedom. It was unusual to have a Japanese-speaking POW – me – in the group, and this was one of the most poignant opportunities I have had to speak about reconciliation.

On returning from Japan I received an email from Word of Life Press in Tokyo. Members of their company had been at one of our Agape rallies and had been struck by my testimony. They wanted to publish a book. Would I return to Japan for three weeks of interviews? Over the next year Mrs Emiko Yuki and I worked on the manuscript, me telling my story while she composed the Japanese text. *Take the Torch Shining in the Dark* was published in February 2005.[64] Numerous Japanese have written to me saying how encouraged they have been through reading it.

In April 2006 my home phone rang and I found myself speaking with Aomori's TV station. They had a copy of *Take the Torch* and wanted me to record a programme for them. It transpired that the head of their TV company had visited a local university professor to chat about Eric Liddell. This professor had come to Evelyn's Sunday school class back in 1958 and had just received an advert for the book, which he quickly retrieved from his waste-paper basket!

"Will you come to Japan in the cherry blossom season?"

"Perhaps autumn will be better?" I protested. The cherry blossom season was two weeks away.

The lady was persistent. She rang three times to persuade me that her project was worth doing and that cherry blossom would be a far better backdrop. And so I returned to Japan once more. Remarkably, on my flight from Aomori to Tokyo, I found myself sitting with the university professor. He and another man from Evelyn's Sunday school class had read *Take the Torch* and attended a meeting I spoke at. As a result, both of them had rededicated their lives to God. He also told me that the head of the university had come to my Bible classes in the early 1960s and become a Christian while a junior high schoolboy in one of the fishing villages on the Aomori coast. This man had also read my book and was telling his students that, just as I had passed on Eric Liddell's baton of forgiveness to him, he was passing the baton on to them.

And so it goes on. Through my friendship with Eric Liddell, the book, and TV and radio programmes, valuable opportunities to testify of God's grace still arise from time to time. But I have got ahead of myself, and this is not where this story really finishes.

引|継ぎ

Hikitsugi
(Take the Torch)

On Sunday, 14 August 2005 I awoke from a deep sleep and was instinctively drawn to the windows of my hotel room. I pulled back the curtain and gazed out onto a sight that I had not seen for sixty-three years. There were the familiar lines of the harbour shores, the Bluff and the islands of Chefoo. To the far right was the hinterland; an untouched skyline. Every curve and crag, every ridge and ravine was no different than I remembered it. Here was a memory I had never mislaid, that had lain dormant and now had been awakened. Below me, however, my old-world town of less than 200,000 had been displaced by the wide roads and high rises of a city with over one and a half million people.[65] I suddenly felt empathy with Urashima Taro, Japan's counterpart to Rip van Winkle.

I had arrived in Chefoo, from the summer heat and urban smog of Beijing, at midnight, accompanied by Neil Yorkston and two of his daughters, Catherine and Ruth. Evelyn had stayed at home for this trip. It was Neil, my old Chefoo school friend, who had encouraged me to come to China.

"There are a whole group of ex-Chefusians going," he told me on the phone. "The Shandong authorities are organizing three days of celebration. It will be sixty years since our liberation. Why don't you come along? I want to go down south and see Guizhou Province again. You could go on to Yunnan."

China revisited was a strange experience. The "sing-song" nature of the language seemed as familiar as the characters that faced every street-sign, billboard, shop-front and banknote. But I was around fifteen seconds behind in every conversation, hanging on to a smattering of half-remembered words and losing everything in translation. Comprehending the script was akin to viewing examples of chiaroscuro; words which meant the same in Chinese and Japanese helped me on my way, but those that didn't left me in the dark.

After breakfast our group was ferried by bus to church. When we left Chefoo in 1942 four of the local pastors were in prison for refusing to hang Hirohito's picture in the sanctuary and bow to it. The grandson of one of the four was now the minister. The congregation had suffered persecution in the long Mao years but the church, as is the case across China, was now flourishing. The building seemed ready to burst as we entered. Only red-taped bureaucracy was holding up the congregation's desire to demolish the existing structure and construct a new and larger one. This was one of three services that day.

"Do you know the meaning of *A-men*?" I asked our non-Christian Chinese guide. The Chinese word sounds the same as the English.

"It is a religious word," she said seriously. "I am not familiar with its meaning. I will find out for you."

Gratifyingly, the pastor provided her, not me, with a lengthy explanation.

With modernization of the city, little of our past remained intact. As we toured around, we relied on our collective memory to conjure up images of bumpy lanes, crooked alleyways, colonnaded footpaths, strait-laced facades along shopping streets and majestic houses protected by imposing walls. Chefoo School was still there, now an academy for the navy. We wandered in and out of the buildings recalling the individuals, staff and students, who had by degrees enriched or perhaps, we joked, blighted our lives. Sadly, the foundation stones had been defaced by zealous Communists and phrases such as "the faithfulness of God" had been obliterated. After a multi-course banquet provided by local government officials, we reminisced well into an agreeable evening.

The visit to Weifang internment camp was an outstanding event, choreographed with unerring proficiency by our hosts. It seemed everything was in contrast to the hardship of our past experiences. We travelled by luxury coach, not basic boat and train, along *gaosu gonglu* – high-speed freeways. The journey took three hours from Chefoo, not forty-eight. As honoured guests we were accommodated in a four-star hotel where an army of active staff were continually on watch to meet every request of their elderly charges. For three days we were the centre of attention, not the inconvenient chattels of an occupying militia. We were fêted by government officials, surrounded by clusters of curious onlookers, encircled by national and international media.

The little walled city of Weifang had gone, replaced by a packed metropolis now famous for its annual international kite-flying festival. The cityscape had been pushed out way beyond the original walls, absorbing the area occupied by the camp well within its suburbs. The original site had, in part, been transformed into the city's No. 2 Middle School. Only nine of the original buildings seem to have survived: a ladies' dormitory, the men's accommodation, Shadyside Hospital and three of the Wall Street terraces in front of it. The three others had been in the Japanese compound. One of these, the Japanese General Stores, was to become the "Weifang Concentration Camp Memorial Museum". I left them a copy of *Take the Torch* to add to their exhibits.

A small memorial park had been laid out in front of what had been the main gate and the river was being re-routed and deepened to allow boats to dock there. At the centre of the park is an impressive monument: a four-sided obelisk bearing sculpted birds, flying free above life-sized figures of an American and a Chinese soldier mingling with released internees and liberated Chinese. Facing the monument there is a cast bronze relief depicting internees at work. One of the figures carries a picture with a likeness of Eric Liddell. Nor far away, by one of the old terraced blocks, stands a seven-foot-high slab of red granite brought from the Isle of Mull in Scotland, a tribute to Eric dedicated in 1991. On the back it bears a brief obituary in Chinese and English inscribed in gold. On the front is a fitting text: "They shall mount up with wings as eagles; they shall run and not be weary."[66]

I had been asked belatedly to prepare the "Eric Liddell Memorial Speech" at the official celebration of our liberation, on Wednesday 17 August 2005. It had to be strictly no longer than three minutes and must in no circumstances contain any political or religious comment. In the hotel at Chefoo I had rushed down to the office and asked to borrow a computer. It took me 90 minutes to produce that 180-second talk! The formalities came on the second day of our stay in Weifang. One thousand five hundred pigeons were released, the birds representing the internees, and then a battery of fireworks exploded into miniature parachutes which symbolized our American liberators.

As a crowd gathered around Eric's memorial a bureaucrat, eager to throw his weight around, pounced on my speech.

"It is more than three minutes. We must cancel it."

"Oh, no," the organizing secretary came over and took my notes. "It is fine," he said after a few moments. "It will not be too long. Perhaps a few adjustments…" To spare his colleague's "face" he quickly altered one or two words in the opening remarks and stood back.

It was raining gently as the interpreter and I began. I was pleased that the Chinese crowd stayed to listen.

"Eric gave me two things," I told them. "His worn-out running shoes. My own shoes had worn out and it was mid-winter… The best thing he gave me was his 'baton of forgiveness'. He taught me to love my enemies, the Japanese, and to pray for them. In 1952, I went to Japan by ship. The ship was carrying 300 young British soldiers. On Sunday, their officer asked me to speak to the soldiers. I told them the story of Eric Liddell and how he had taught me to love my enemies. I told them, 'You are going to Korea with guns and may die there fighting with the UN for peace. I am going to Japan with Eric's message of True Peace.'"

As I spoke, I was also thinking of my school friend, Brian Thompson. The neglected burial mounds in that remote corner of the compound have long since disappeared beneath new building-sites. I paid my own silent tribute to him and comforted myself with the thought that God knows where we laid him and Eric to rest, and he will raise them when Jesus returns.[67]

Afterwards Shandong Television requested a forty-minute interview. I included all the religious and political matters I had avoided in the original speech. When I asked how the footage would be used, the interviewer simply said that they would broadcast it when they needed to.

After the speech Neil and I wandered over to Shadyside Hospital. Neil had persuaded someone to open up the third-floor attic for us. It was a peculiar feeling mounting the stone steps to the grey brick entrance and then climbing the stairs to my old bedroom. Instinctively I turned right along the corridor and began recalling the names of those who had slept there. The room was completely bare. We pulled open one of the dark-red framed dormer windows and waved to friends below. These were the same three windows that Hummel and Tipton had looked out of as they planned their escape in 1944. There had been a commanding view over the boundary wall – beyond the barbed wire and the electric fence, the guard tower and the trench – across the river to the open fields and, for us, the new occupants of their vacated room, to fantasies of escape. But it was idle talk. We were young then. As I gazed out towards our coach waiting on the river bridge to take us back to the luxury of our hotel and the pleasure of yet another banquet, those distressing days all seemed so long ago.

帰国
Kikoku
(Return Home)

Two days later my plane settled into its approach to Wujiabao Airport after a three-hour flight from Shandong Province, and I caught my first glimpse of Kunming since 1945. Like Chefoo and Weifang, the city had grown enormously, pushing its precincts into the hills that guard the routes to the north, east and west, its expansion south blocked by the polluted turquoise waters of Lake Dian. My eyes, however, were more drawn to the tribal hills of the north, where I would be heading the next morning. Here, nestled out of sight, I would find Taku again. I had been eleven the last Christmas holiday I had spent there. That was sixty-seven years ago.

Wherever I travelled in China, the Chinese penchant for billboards, building-sites and skyscrapers seemed indefatigable. Kunming was no different. The airport, one of the oldest in China and once on the periphery of the city, was now stubbornly stuck within its urban setting. A fluorescent-red, three-wheeled taxi delivered me to my hotel. As we trundled through the streets I was again aware how few of my memories correlated with modern China. This century, the publicity says, is to be China's and it was clear that the Chinese were wasting little time in establishing their claim to urban prosperity. Where once tens of motor vehicles had ruled the Kunming roads, now my little taxi puttered perilously in and out of thousands of private cars, public buses, trucks, bicycles, hand-carts and pedestrians, all apparently eager to claim their space on the twenty-first-century highway. At my hotel I was warned of another hazard. It was best to keep my room phone off the hook; otherwise I may be troubled by prostitutes.

The following day I travelled to Wuding, around forty miles north-west, accompanied by an interpreter and a Christian Chinese guide. Wuding was the home of Wang Zhiming, a Miao church leader martyred during the Cultural Revolution, whom I knew as a child. I met him when my parents attended a meeting of Chinese pastors and missionaries at Sapushan, the centre for Miao work, which is located on top of a mountain, half a day's walk north from Wuding. Wang Zhiming's statue now graces one of the ten alcoves above the west doors of Westminster Abbey in a memorial to innocent victims of oppression, violence and war.

Until we escaped Kunming, every crossroad seemed to be a log-jam needing to be prised open by our bus driver with the incessant blast of the horn. Ahead of us lay the first steep climb out of the city. We plunged into a mile-long tunnel, a dark corridor of stifling pollution, the way ahead only dimly illuminated by headlights. When we finally emerged from the murky depths of the mountain we were in countryside. Landscapes that I still recognized opened up at every curve in the road and at the cresting of each summit. Now, at last, I felt I was on familiar, unchanged ground.

Our vehicle from Wuding to Taku was a buff, soft-topped Beijing Jeep Company land-rover and we needed every torque of its four-wheel drive. The head of the Wuding Religious Affairs Bureau proved to be a very skilful driver and his deputy, remarkably, turned out to be the grandson of Xiao Yang, my old playmate in Taku. Our route varied from well-laid tarmac to dire stretches of rough road where thousands of stones had been driven into the dirt. Signposts were conspicuous by their general absence. We plunged into fast-running rivers and scraped up and down ruts that jeopardized the chassis. Around us the mountains seemed to rise to the skies, one range after another. The lower slopes were covered with acres of corn, an assortment of vegetables and fields of broad-leafed tobacco plants. Terraces of sunflowers brightened the route. Small flocks of black goats grazed in the most improbable of places. We climbed, passing through dozens of tribal villages of no more than thirty or forty houses, to 8,000 feet and then descended around a series of needle-sharp hairpin bends before climbing again.

After five hours of lurching from side to side and jumping in our seats over every lump and bump, our land-rover rounded a bend in the road and there, on the mountain ledge where I had left it, was Taku. Little seemed to have changed. Unimportant in the world, the village and its people had been bypassed. It was three hours' walk to a bus stop and only one bus a day came that way. The little white church, with the cross painted on its gable, still stood at the end of the path, surrounded by a field of ripening maize. The village was larger, but not significantly so. Slowly we negotiated the final twelve hairpin bends, some so tight that we needed to back up to get around them. Waiting for me was Xiao Yang in his grey flat cap and old-fashioned Mao jacket, a great toothless grin on his face – the same wide smile he had worn as a child. The pastor and his wife took me by the arms and guided me forward. Tears filled my eyes. On a path above the road were lines of young children, dressed in their best clothes, shyly waving at me. Two young men had stretched a yellow banner edged in red over the path. In Chinese and English it read: "A warm welcome to a dear family member coming home."[68]

On my left were women of the village, arrayed in all the colour and splendour of their native dress – intricately embroidered pastel pink, green and blue layered tunics, over plain cotton trousers with broad bands of embroidery at the ankles. Some wore ornate slippers and all of them wore elaborate peaked bonnets bedecked with flowers over their long tresses of striking black hair. Opposite stood the men, more soberly attired, though some had donned black jackets edged with tassels and displaying the same dexterity in the needlework patterns threaded along the seams. This was the choir. Led by the strong baritone voice of the choir-master and accompanied on the accordion, they sang their rich welcome, keeping rhythm with their clapping. The splendour of their melody matched their clothing. Their harmonies rang out over the tiled roofs of their homes, across the lush greenness of their valley and echoed back from the hills. The music reached deep within me and like a key, unlocked my emotions. I was overwhelmed. My cheeks ran with tears. It was such a beautiful thing. They, the Eastern Lisu, were singing for me.

Without missing a beat, the choir-master and his wife took my arm and, as the choir formed a procession in front of me, I was led down through the village to the church. The barn-like interior with its green and white walls, square-panelled ceiling and round wooden columns was as I remembered it. The low-backed wooden benches were new. As were the fluorescent lighting strip, a makeshift chandelier and a silver-faced clock mounted behind the grey wooden desk that served as the pastor's lectern. Either side of the central red cross painted on the wall were banners reading from top to bottom

– "Rock of Ages cleft for me... Let me hide myself in Thee."[69]
I was surprised to find myself speaking into a microphone. I
told the crowded church what had happened to my parents,
encouraged them in their faith and thanked them for their
very moving welcome.

This meeting was quickly brought to a close and we
were hurried across to a courtyard where a feast had been
prepared. We sat in the open air around circular tables and
were served with bowls of rice and choice dishes of cabbage,
root vegetables, offal and innards, pork and chicken. I was
honoured with a rotund, ripe pomegranate from a tree my
father had planted. I brought out photographs that had been
taken in the 1930s and there was much laughter as the older
folk recognized themselves or relatives. A group of young
men appeared with a dilapidated accordion, an old trunk and
a large battered cooking-pot that had belonged to my family.
I was amazed they had kept them for so many years, but they
told me that they treasured them as their only remaining
reminders of my parents.

My old home was still there, now owned by a Christian
family who had bought it from the government. The balcony
was hidden beneath rows of drying tobacco leaves strung
along wooden poles and a large satellite dish on a metal tripod
dominated the front veranda! The doors and the yellow panels
either side of the small barred windows had been painted
with pictures of flowers and trees. The layout was the same
as it had always been, but with the stairs now removed to the
outside of the building. That evening, I lay in bed listening
to the familiar, though now incomprehensible, chatter of
the villagers in the room below. The hillsides hummed with
sounds of the night, evoking fresh memories of my childhood.

The mountain air was cold, but my exhaustion from the day's travel quickly pulled me into much-needed sleep.

I was awakened by the incessant crowing of cockerels and the pleasing aroma of early-morning wood-fires. Breakfast is not an event as far as the Eastern Lisu are concerned, and I was ushered down to the local school to give out presents of colouring books and pencils to the pupils. The church service which followed lasted over three hours. The building was packed. The men sat on the left and the women to the right. This Sunday was their celebration of the one hundredth anniversary of the arrival of their Pastor, Wang Huairen, my father, in China.[70] People had travelled great distances. One old man had walked for eight hours to be there.

"When Pastor Wang visited our village, he always stayed in my home," he told me proudly.

Once again I was treated to the most evocative hymn singing, the worship pouring out of the building in praise to God. There were choirs from other villages; even from a Han Chinese village where recently twenty families had turned to Christ and destroyed their idol shelves. It was wonderful to realize that these poor, often despised, tribal people are reaching out to their Han Chinese neighbours. I was asked to preach, my message translated first into Mandarin and then Eastern Lisu. But for the most part I was content to sit and listen to the beautiful hymns of praise and the whispered prayers of old friends.

After the service I was led through the crowds. A beautiful moon gate[71] had been formed out of greenery, pine boughs twisted together with branches of beech. I was given a traditional embroidered *jeeka* bag to hang over my shoulder and a man offered me an Eastern Lisu hymn-book. Some of the older people who had said goodbye to my father and mother now gathered to let me go. They told me that I was the first "outsider" to visit them since my parents left. I saw the depth of their affection for my family in their faces as I said my farewell. Now I could truly appreciate what my father, with the help of my mother, had achieved. Then I stepped through the moon gate and glanced back at the intricate interweaving of colour behind me. It was like a tapestry of my life.

Afterword

The Eastern Lisu and the Work of George "Eddie" Metcalf (1906–51)

At the Religious Affairs Bureau offices at Wuding in Yunnan Province is a translation of the New Testament. It is a heavy, dark-blue volume measuring approximately fifteen by twenty-three centimetres. On the first page is my father's signature above the initials "CIM" and the date "Dec 51", the year he and my mother left China for the final time. Beneath this is an inscription in Chinese and Lisu script explaining a point of translation. It was my dad's personal copy and one that carries his notes and reflections. My sister, Ruth, inherited this copy when my mother died and in 1999 she sent it to China where it properly belongs.

Eddie began his final translation work of the New Testament in earnest when ill-health curtailed his ability to undertake the arduous walks across the mountains to visit remote Eastern Lisu villages. However, his engagement with developing a written language for these people had begun much earlier. In 1910 he and an Australian missionary, Arthur Nicholls, another China Inland Mission worker, adapted a script developed for the Miao people by Samuel Pollard, a Methodist missionary. Two years later they produced the first written script and between 1912 and 1936 portions of the Bible were published.

In 1951, under the scrutiny of Chinese Communist officials, Eddie carried his precious New Testament translation through innumerable checks of his baggage out to Hong Kong, where it was published. Copies exist in some libraries, but, sadly, with the closing of China and the internal hostility to Christianity, the edition could never be transported back to Yunnan to be used by the men and women Eddie had painstakingly translated it for.

The Eastern Lisu, or Eastern Lipo as they are also known, are found in north central Yunnan, particularly around Wuding and Yuanmou (the nearest town to Taku for my father and mother), and in small communities in south Sichuan Province. The Eastern Lisu originally lived alongside the Lisu in the Salween River Valley, north-west Yunnan, but moved to the mountainous Wuding region around 1812 after being defeated in battle. Under the national minority classification of the Chinese government, they are now associated with the Yi Minority peoples. They have, however, more in common with the Lisu historically and linguistically, and for local administrative affairs are considered part of the Lisu Minority.

Arthur Nicholls started missionary work amongst the tribal people of the Wuding region of north Yunnan Province in October 1906, the same month in which Eddie arrived in China (23 October) for language study. In 1908 Nicholls was joined by Eddie and, while Nicholls concentrated on the Miao people at Sapushan, Eddie, gradually, committed himself to work amongst the Eastern Lisu around Taku.

Caught up in a culture of alcohol abuse, opium addiction, folk religion and illiteracy, the north Yunnan Minority tribes responded rapidly to the gospel and in great numbers in the early 1900s. Churches were built and regular services started. Outreach between tribes also drew people to faith in Jesus. Eddie witnessed the conversion of literally thousands of tribal people to Christianity. He constructed the church and founded a Bible College at Taku, and he ran a dispensary in our home.

When Eddie and Bessie departed from Taku in 1951, they left behind a strong Christian community. The church, however, was closed down and their Bible portions and hymn-books were burned. The Bible College, along with others in the area, was demolished. For the next thirty years the church suffered persecution. The leaders were imprisoned in labour camps and some of them died for their faith. Since the Cultural Revolution, with the recognition of Protestant Christianity as one of China's five official religions, the church has again grown rapidly. Today there are over 70,000 Eastern Lisu believers.[72]

In 2005, after my return from Yunnan, I received a letter from Simon Wong of the Hong Kong Bible Society. He was the adviser to a group of local Eastern Lisu involved in a translation of the Bible for their own people. The translators had assembled at the Trinity International Church in Kunming and were producing a new translation based on the Chinese Union Bible and using, among other resources, my father's translation. On 1 October 2009, as this book was being prepared for publication, the United Bible Societies posted news on their website that the Eastern Lisu New Testament has now been successfully published and distributed.[73]

Author's Notes

In this book the Eastern Lisu are referred to either by this name or by a shortened form, "Lisu". This is entirely for convenience in writing and there is no implication that the Eastern Lisu and Lisu Minorities are one and the same.

Generally Chinese names have been rendered in modern Pinyin romanization, apart from Chefoo and the Yangtze River, which in English are better known by these terms. The name of the village in Yunnan where Steve lived as a child, Taku, is the romanized form used at the time.

It has not been possible to interview everyone whose stories have been shared with Steve's and therefore this book represents his recollection of events. There are no invented characters in the story, but some names have been changed to protect identity. Reported conversations convey the essence of what was said, not verbatim accounts. The interpretation of facts and the style of presentation remain my responsibility.

Ronald Clements

Bibliography

China

A History of Christian Missions in China, by Kenneth Scott Latourette, Society for Promoting Christian Knowledge, 1929

"A Province at War: Guangxi during the Sino-Japanese Conflict, 1937–45", by Graham Hitchings, *The China Quarterly*, December 1986

"A Song of Salvation at Weihsien Prison Camp", by Mary Previte, *Philadelphia Inquirer*, 25 August 1985

Chefoo School 1881–1951, by Gordon Martin, Braunton, Devon: Merlin Books, 1990

China: the Reluctant Exodus, by Phyllis Thompson, Sevenoaks: Hodder & Stoughton and OMF, 1979

"Chronological Report on Duck Mission", by William G. Norwood, 7 September 1945

Courtyard of the Happy Way, by Norman Cliff, Arthur James Ltd, 1977

Eric Liddell: Pure Gold, by David McCasland, Grand Rapids, USA: Discovery House Publishers, 2001

History of U.S. Marine Corps: Operations in World War II, Volume V: Victory and Occupation, by Benis M. Frank and Henry I. Shaw, Jr, Historical Branch, U.S. Marine Corps, 1968

Hudson Taylor in Early Years – The Growth of a Soul, by Dr and Mrs Howard Taylor, London: Morgan and Scott, 1911

Lilla's Feast, by Frances Osborne, London: Doubleday, Transworld Publishers, 2004

Operation China, by Paul Hattaway, Carlisle: Piquant and Global Mapping International, CD-ROM edition, 2002

Region and Nation: The Kwangsi Clique in Chinese Politics 1925–1937, by Diana Lary, Cambridge Studies in Chinese History, Literature and Institutions, Cambridge University Press, 1974

"Report on the accident which resulted in the death of Francis Brian Thompson, August 16th 1944", Weihsien, 1944

Running the Race: Eric Liddell, Olympic Champion and Missionary, by John W. Keddie, Evangelical Press, 2007

Shandung Compound, by Langdon Gilkey, San Francisco: HarperCollins Publishers, 1966

"Strategy of the Sino-Japanese War", by Fordyce Carlson Evans, *Far Eastern Survey*, American Council of the Institute of Pacific Relations, Vol. X, No. 15, 11 August 1941

The Boxer Uprising, by V. Purcell, Cambridge University Press, 1963

The Jubilee Story of the China Inland Mission, by Marshall Broomhall, London: Morgan and Scott, 1915

The North China Herald and Supreme Court and Consular Gazette, Shanghai, 7 October 1936

Japan

50 Years of Silence, by Jan Ruff-O'Herne, Sydney / Amsterdam / New York: Tom Thompson, 1994

"90 suicides a day spur Japan into action", by Leo Lewis, *The Times*, 12 November 2007

A Century of Protestant Christianity in Japan, by Charles W. Iglehart, Vermont, USA: Charles E. Tuttle, 1959

"A Needy Field", by Mary Milner, *The Millions*, CIM, Australia, May 1954

A Passion for the Impossible, by Leslie Lyall, OMF Publications, 1965

"A Red Letter Day", by Lorna Edwards, *The Millions*, CIM, Australia, July 1956

Beyond Death and Dishonour, by Michiharu Shinya, translated by Eric H. Thompson, Auckland, New Zealand: Castle Publishing, 2001

Captives of the Mighty, by Dorothy Pape, London: CIM/OMF, 1959

City Life in Japan: A Study of a Tokyo Ward, by R. P. Dore, Berkeley and Los Angeles: University of California Press, 1958

"Collectivity and agency in remembering and reconciliation", by David Middleton and Kyoko Murakami, *Outlines*, No. 1, 2003

"Early Experiences", by Shirley Tamsitt, *The Millions*, CIM, Australia, July 1957

"Hirohito Is Enthroned As Japan's Ruler", *Syracuse Herald*, 11 November 1928

"Hirohito shunned war criminal shrine", by Justin McCurry, *The Guardian*, 20 July 2006

Hiroshima – Three Witnesses, by Hara Tamiki, Ota Yoko, and Toge Sankichi, edited and translated by Richard H. Minear, New Jersey: Princeton University Press, 1990

"If it be Thou...", by Frank Houghton, *China's Millions*, CIM, Australia, March 1951

"Imperial Rescript to Soldiers and Sailors", Japan, 4 January 1882

"Japan dismisses 'comfort women' apology", by Leo Lewis, *The Times*, 28 June 2007

"Japan faces storm over 'rewriting' war history", by Leo Lewis, *The Times*, 6 April 2005

"Let Us Go On", by J. Oswald Sanders, Supplement to *China's Millions*, CIM, Australia, 15 December 1951

My Lucky Life – in War, Revolution, Peace & Diplomacy, by Sir Sam Falle, Isis Publishing, 2004

"Our Stake in Japan", by W. G. Searle, *The Millions*, CIM, Australia, April 1954

"POW Camps in Japan Proper", by Toru Fukubayashi, translated by Yuka Ibuki, POW Research Network Japan, www.powersearch.jp

Prisoners of the Japanese, by Gavin Daws, London: Simon & Schuster UK, 2006

Shadows of Hiroshima, by Wilfred Burchett, London: Verso Editions, 1983

Shinto and the State 1868–1988, by Helen Hardacre, Princeton University Press, 1989

"Snow and Blossom", by Dorothy Garnham, *The Millions*, CIM, Australia, October 1956

Take off your Shoes, by Michael Griffiths, London: OMF, 1971

Testimonies of CIM (OMF) Missionaries, OMF internal publication, 1998

The Campaigns of MacArthur in the Pacific, Volume I, prepared by General Douglas MacArthur's general staff, facsimile reprint 1994, first printed Tokyo, 1950

"The Future of the Inland Mission", by Frank Houghton, *China's Millions*, CIM, Australia, February 1951

The Japanese Mind: The Goliath Explained, by Robert C. Christopher, New York: Linden Press, Simon & Schuster, 1983

"The Roots of Subservience", by Kan Takayuki, *AMPO Japan-Asia Quarterly Review*, Vol. 20, No. 3, 1989

"What a Language!", by Mary Milner, *The Millions*, CIM, Australia, August 1954

Winners in Peace: MacArthur, Yoshida, and Postwar Japan, by Richard B. Finn, University of California Press, 1992

"Woman calls British ex-POWs to Japan", by Iain Ball, *Japan Times*, 20 February 2002

Korea

The Korean War, by Max Hastings, London: Book Club Associates by arrangement with Michael Joseph, 1987

Websites

http://news.bbc.co.uk/1/hi/uk/1168149.stm   (BBC)

http://fpcj.jp/old/e/mres/publication/ff/pdf_07/02_population.pdf   (Foreign Press Center, Japan)

http://news.bbc.co.uk/1/hi/england/somerset/2986762.stm (BBC)

www.agape-reconciliation.org/testimony.htm   (Agape)

www.anbhf.org/laureates/htaylor.html   (American National Business Hall of Fame)

www.army.mil/CMH/books/wwii/MacArthur%20Reports/MacArthur%20V1/ch12.htm   (US Army Center of Military History)

www.cia.gov/library/publications/the-world-factbook/geos/ja.html   (CIA World Factbook)

www.city.sendai.jp/kikaku/kokusai/english/kankou.html (Sendai)

www.combinedfleet.com/btl_jav.htm   (Imperial Japanese Navy Page)

www.joshuaproject.net/peopctry.php   (Joshua Project)

www.jref.com/glossary/emperor_hirohito_showa.shtml   (Japan Reference)

www.pcf.city.hiroshima.jp   (Hiroshima Peace Site)

www.powresearch.jp/en/pdf_e/powlist/nagoya/nagoya_4b_iruka_e_001.pdf   (POW Research Network Japan)

www.sil.org/asia/ldc/plenary_papers/david_bradley.pdf   (SIL International)

www.state.gov/r/pa/ho/time/cwr/91194.htm   (US Department of State)

http://www.ubscp.org/eastlisu-nt   (United Bible Societies China Partnership)

www.yantai-life.com/yantaifacts.htm   (Yantai-Life)

www.yasukuni.or.jp/english/about/index.html   (Yasukuni Shrine)

Notes

1. Max Hastings, *The Korean War*, London: Book Club Associates by arrangement with Michael Joseph, 1987.
2. Taku is now known as 滘谷, Taogu.
3. Referred to hereafter either as Eastern Lisu or simply "Lisu". This latter term should not be confused with other Lisu in China who are distinct people groups.
4. Psalm 23:1, 4, KJV.
5. The Treaty Ports were harbours where Western powers and Japan gained significant "rights" of jurisdiction and trade following victories over China. Chefoo was established as a Treaty Port in 1858 under the Treaty of Tianjin.
6. Both hymns by Frank Houghton, 1930 and 1934 © OMF International. Frank Houghton was General Director of CIM, 1940–51, and the brother of Stanley Houghton, one of the Chefoo teachers.
7. *The Crucifixion* by John Stainer, words selected and written by Revd William John Sparrow-Simpson, 1887.
8. While the China Inland Mission school in Chefoo did close in 1942, never to be reopened, CIM/OMF subsequently started "Chefoo Schools" in other areas of China and overseas. The last of the "Chefoo Schools" was in the Cameron Highlands of Malaysia and closed in 2001.
9. The importance of maintaining one's "face" (or that of others) is a very strong cultural trait in Asian societies, tied to feelings of shame. Wherever possible, being shamed or shaming others is to be avoided.
10. Kittie Louise Jennett Suffield, 1929.
11. A map of the Weifang (Weihsien) POW camp can be found at http://www.weihsien-paintings.org/maps/indexFrame.htm
12. In *Courtyard of the Happy Way* (Arthur James Ltd, 1977),

Norman Cliff reports seeing prisoner totals of 1,492 and 1,518 on consecutive days.

13. "Report on the accident which resulted in the death of Francis Brian Thompson August 16th 1944", compiled by members of the Weishien (Weifang) Internees General Committee, 29 August 1944, and private communication with Neil Yorkston, July 2008. Other published versions of this story indicate that one of the boys present challenged Brian to touch the electric cable. From the official accident report it is clear that these versions are not correct and that this was a tragic accident.

14. Hummel became an American Ambassador to China, 1981–85. His escape from the Japanese and aid for the Chinese guerrillas apparently stood him in good stead!

15. Milton Ager and Jack Yellen, 1929.

16. Richard Rogers and Oscar Hammerstein II, 1943.

17. 中國內地會

18. Now Netaji Subhash Chandra Bose International Airport.

19. Now the Raj Bhavan.

20. Private communication with John Sampson, Victorian Baptist Historical Society, Kew Baptist Church, Melbourne, August 2008.

21. At the time of this voyage a ceasefire was still eight months ahead. The total UN armed services death toll was 451,692 with 546,602 wounded. In the last 24 days of fighting the UN sustained 17,000 casualties, with 3,333 dead. In 33 months of engagement China, with her policy of "human wave" tactics – the Chinese forces would attack with rank after rank of soldiers storming a UN position, in an attempt to overrun it by sheer weight of numbers – lost between half a million and one and a half million soldiers in total.

22. In the 1930s Beihai was known as Pakhoi and was in Guangdong Province, not Guangxi Province as it is now. This incident may have taken place in 1937. Japan made a number of attacks on the south China coast, including attacks on Beihai, during this period. In 1936 a Japanese medicine merchant, Nakano, was murdered in the town and Japan used this incident to apply pressure on the provincial government. This sporadic belligerence finally allowed the Japanese to land

a force at Beihai in November 1939 and march north to seize the provincial capital, Nanning.

23. This openness to importing foreign ideas and industry has not always been present. For a long period, during the Tokugawa Shogunate (1639–1853), the country shunned contact with the world, to the extent of restricting the size of ships, thus preventing its population straying too far. Foreign trade was confined to the solitary port of Nagasaki where merchants from overseas were holed up as humiliated inmates. Native sailors swept away from their home shores and washed up on foreign beaches were not allowed to return.

24. *San* is a title showing respect, added to the name of an adult, male or female. It can also be added to a person's occupation title.

25. Some commentators see Japanese society in terms of the roles of males and females as much more nuanced, with females dominating the home environment and having a profound influence on both male and female children. There have, of course, also been many changes in Japanese society since the 1950s.

26. The Japanese word for "cry" and "chirp", *naku*, I later discovered, is the same spoken word but written differently.

27. *The Land of Beulah* by Jefferson Haskel, 1860.

28. 2 Corinthians 8:2–3, NIV.

29. John 8:7, KJV.

30. After World War II SCAP (Supreme Commander of the Allied Powers), an organization headed by General Douglas MacArthur, was created in Japan to oversee military, political and social developments. While it was an initiative of the Allied powers, it was almost entirely run by the USA. SCAP's work was "the initial effort to punish and reform Japan, the work to revive the Japanese economy, and the conclusion of a formal peace treaty and alliance". A peace treaty was signed 8 September 1951 and became effective 28 April 1952, ending the Allied occupation of Japan and re-establishing Japan's autonomy over her own affairs.

31. On Sunday, 26 September 1954 the *Toya Maru* sank in the Tsugaru Straits with a reported loss of 1,153 passengers and

crew. Four other ferries were also sunk. This incident led to
the construction in 1971, completed 1988, of the 54-kilometre
Seikan Tunnel linking the islands of Honshu and Hokkaido,
the longest undersea tunnel in the world.

32. *Sensei*, a term of respect for teachers and those who have
mastered some skill or art.

33. Now the United Society for the Propagation of the Gospel,
renamed in 1965.

34. Exodus 4:11–12, NIV.

35. 王怀仁 – *Wang* is the surname, *Huai* means "to cherish" and
Ren means "benevolent".

36. Carl G. Gowman, American missionary (1886–1930), with
his wife and daughter, joined Eddie Metcalf in his work at
Taku. They later parted company over the issue of baptism by
immersion.

37. Letter from Eddie Metcalf, 25 March 1920 (with added note, 1
November 1920), SOAS archives CIM/PP, Section 4, File 136,
FHT notes.

38. Letter from Elizabeth Metcalf, 28 February 1927, SOAS
archives CIM /PP, Section 4, File 136, FHT notes.

39. As used in Psalm 19:1.

40. As used to describe the Holy Spirit, the "Paraclete".

41. 2 Timothy 2:3, KJV.

42. OMF at that time worked on a three-month remittance scheme,
whereby missionaries got a share of donations made in the
previous three months.

43. Psalm 84:11, KJV.

44. Matthew 5:8, KJV.

45. Genesis 1:1, KJV.

46. "I am less sanguine than many others, but it is my confident
belief that if the missionary societies are faithful to their
charge up to the end of this century you need not after 1890
send any more missionaries to Japan... The finishing of the
work can be safely left to the foreign force which will by that
time be there, working in conjunction with the ever increasing
number of native pastors and evangelists. Some put 1890
as the date, some 1895, but no one puts it later than 1900"
(Guido Verbeck). "It is not an extravagant anticipation that

Japan may become a Christian nation in seventeen years. The Christian missionaries in Japan are now working with a strong hope that the twentieth century will open upon that island empire no longer a foreign mission field but predominantly Christian" (Christian editorial, 1883). Both extracts quoted in *Take off your Shoes* by Michael Griffiths, London: OMF, 1971, pp. 25–26.

47. Romans 11:29, NIV.

48. 2 Timothy 1:6, KJV.

49. Herbert J. Taylor (1893–1978), one-time President of Rotary International, promoted an ethical code, the Four-way Test, for successful business.

50. Estimated from 1980 (117,060,000) and 1985 (121,049,000) figures; the current population of Japan is approx. 127.5 million.

51. Genesis 1:3, Japanese Classical Version.

52. 天皇 – *Tenno* is the Japanese term for "Emperor", literally "Heavenly King", a term that Japanese Christians are understandably uncomfortable with.

53. So called because the call of the crane can be heard above others and is therefore associated with authority.

54. "The ties between us and our people have always stood upon mutual trust and affection. They do not depend upon mere legend and myths, they are not predicated on the false conception that the Emperor is manifest deity, and that the Japanese people are superior to other races and fated to rule the world." Emperor Hirohito addressing the Japanese Diet, January 1946, quoted in Charles W. Inglehart, *A Century of Protestant Christianity in Japan*, Vermont: Charles E. Tuttle, 1959, p. 275.

55. Imperial Rescript to Soldiers and Sailors, Japan, 4 January 1882.

56. *Beyond Death and Dishonour*, Michiharu Shinya, translated by Eric H. Thompson, Castle Publishing, New Zealand, 2001, p. 21.

57. In 1867 forces allied to the Meiji Emperor (1852–1912) overthrew the isolationist Tokugawa Shogunate that had ruled Japan for over 250 years. The new regime helped Japan

to emerge as the first East Asian industrialized nation and become a strong military force in the region. While rescripts of the Meiji era did not specifically declare the Emperor to be a god, the divine role of the Emperor was re-established and this paved the way for Hirohito to be seen as a god, albeit with a Japanese, not Western, understanding, in the 1930s.

58. Iruka existed as a village in 1944/45. In 1955 it was merged with two other villages to form Kiwa-cho and, as such, "Iruka village" no longer exists. The name is used throughout this chapter to avoid confusion.

59. Re-designated the Nagoya Number 4 Branch Camp, 6 April 1945.

60. Japan began this policy of transporting POWs to Japan in April 1942. Approximately 36,000 men were detained in around 130 camps. Approximately 3,500 POWs died in Japan; at the end of the war there were 32,418 men in 91 camps.

61. For more information about Agape, visit www.agape-reconciliation.org

62. Jan Ruff-O'Herne, *50 Years of Silence*, Sydney / Amsterdam / New York: Tom Thompson, 1994.

63. Luke 23:34, NIV.

64. Japan: Forest Books, 2005, details from http://www.jclglobal. org/bookshop. This is currently only available in Japanese.

65. 200,000 represents the population of Chefoo during the war when the numbers were swollen by people coming into the town. The current population of Yantai, of which Chefoo is now a part, is about 1.6 million (2004).

66. Isaiah 40:31, KJV.

67. There are reports that Eric Liddell's body was exhumed and removed to the Mausoleum of Martyrs in Shijiazhuang, Hebei Province. According to Chinese officials, however, this is not correct.

68. The English actually read, "Welcome to our dear friend go home", which was not the best translation of the Chinese!

69. "Rock of Ages", Augustus M. Toplady, 1776.

70. This celebration was a little early, as my father did not arrive in China until 1906.

71. Moon gates are open, circular "doors", architectural features

found in Chinese and Japanese gardens. Any association of this event with non-Christian interpretations of moon gates is not intended here.

72. Figures produced by www.joshuaproject.net indicate there are around 72,000 Eastern Lisu Christians, of whom 54,000 are evangelical, in a population of 108,000.

73. http://www.ubscp.org/eastlisu-nt/